# Scientific and Technical Means of Distinguishing Between Natural and Other Outbreaks of Disease

T0138038

# NATO Science Series

*A Series presenting the results of activities sponsored by the NATO Science Committee. The Series is published by IOS Press and Kluwer Academic Publishers, in conjunction with the NATO Scientific Affairs Division.*

A. Life Sciences      IOS Press
B. Physics      Kluwer Academic Publishers
C. Mathematical and Physical Sciences      Kluwer Academic Publishers
D. Behavioural and Social Sciences      Kluwer Academic Publishers
E. Applied Sciences      Kluwer Academic Publishers
F. Computer and Systems Sciences      IOS Press

1. Disarmament Technologies      Kluwer Academic Publishers
2. Environmental Security      Kluwer Academic Publishers
3. High Technology      Kluwer Academic Publishers
4. Science and Technology Policy      IOS Press
5. Computer Networking      IOS Press

**NATO-PCO-DATABASE**

The NATO Science Series continues the series of books published formerly in the NATO ASI Series. An electronic index to the NATO ASI Series provides full bibliographical references (with keywords and/or abstracts) to more than 50000 contributions from internatonal scientists published in all sections of the NATO ASI Series.
Access to the NATO-PCO-DATA BASE is possible via CD-ROM "NATO-PCO-DATA BASE" with user-friendly retrieval software in English, French and German (WTV GmbH and DATAWARE Technologies Inc. 1989).

The CD-ROM of the NATO ASI Series can be ordered from: PCO, Overijse, Belgium

**Series 1: Disarmament Technologies – Vol. 35**

# Scientific and Technical Means of Distinguishing Between Natural and Other Outbreaks of Disease

edited by

## Malcolm Dando

## Graham Pearson

Department of Peace Studies,
University of Bradford, England

and

## Bohumir Kriz

Head of the Centre of Epidemiology and Microbiology,
National Institute of Public Health,
Prague, Czech Republic

**Kluwer Academic Publishers**

Dordrecht / Boston / London

Published in cooperation with NATO Scientific Affairs Division

Proceedings of the NATO Advanced Research Workshop on
Scientific and Technical Means of Distinguishing Between Natural and
Other Outbreaks of Disease
Prague, Czech Republic
18–20 October 1998

A C.I.P. Catalogue record for this book is available from the Library of Congress.


ISBN 0-7923-6990-4 (HB)
ISBN 0-7923-6991-2 (PB)

Published by Kluwer Academic Publishers,
P.O. Box 17, 3300 AA Dordrecht, The Netherlands.

Sold and distributed in North, Central and South America
by Kluwer Academic Publishers,
101 Philip Drive, Norwell, MA 02061, U.S.A.

In all other countries, sold and distributed
by Kluwer Academic Publishers,
P.O. Box 322, 3300 AH Dordrecht, The Netherlands.


Printed on acid-free paper

# Table of Contents

vi

# Preface

The editors would like to thank the authors of the papers at the Advanced Research Workshop for their excellent presentations at the workshop and the production of their drafts. We are also indebted to those who have assisted us by retyping drafts into final papers, particularly Mandy Oliver who helped in the final stages of the preparation of this volume.

We would particularly like to acknowledge the help of our colleague Dr Simon Whitby who set the papers into the required camera-ready format and produced the index. Any remaining errors are, of course, our responsibility.


Malcolm Dando                    Graham Pearson                    Bohumir Kriz

# THE IMPORTANCE OF DISTINGUISHING BETWEEN NATURAL AND OTHER OUTBREAKS OF DISEASE

GRAHAM S. PEARSON
*Visiting Professor of International Security,*
*Department of Peace Studies,*
*University of Bradford,*
*Bradford,*
*West Yorkshire BD7 1DP, UK*

## 1. Introduction

The topic of distinguishing between natural and deliberate or accidental outbreaks of disease is central to building international confidence that unusual outbreaks of disease are **not** the result of prohibited activities. The key to solving this problem of distinguishing natural from other outbreaks lies in the scientific and technological evaluation of outbreaks and this is the focus of this ARW entitled "Scientific and Technical Means of Distinguishing Between Natural and Other Outbreaks of Disease". The March 1996 NATO ARW in Budapest entitled "The Technology of Biological Arms Control and Disarmament" concluded that "the BW challenge is closely related to problems in the public health arena, particularly the emergence and re-emergence of infectious diseases. This close relationship can complicate arms control tasks, such as the differentiation between BW use and the natural, if unusual, outbreak of disease." The summary went on to identify as a short term scientific and technological priority the finding of "a politically acceptable framework for investigations of alleged BW use in the context of the growing public health crisis in many parts of the world as well as the need to develop effective measures for enhancing confidence in compliance with the BWC grounded in the best possible science and technology."

This NATO ARW will address the priority issue identified by the March 1996 NATO ARW in Budapest in the context of the current approaches being considered as measures to strengthen the Biological and Toxin Weapons Convention[1] (BTWC) by the Ad Hoc Group currently meeting in Geneva. It is noted that the importance of the work of this Ad Hoc Group in strengthening the BTWC was stressed by the NATO Heads of State and Government at their meeting in Madrid in July 1997 when they said[2] that:

> Recognising that enhancing confidence in compliance would
> reinforce the Biological and Toxin Weapons Convention, we reaffirm
> our determination to complete as soon as possible through negotiation
> a legally binding and effective verification mechanism.

As the manifestation of use of a biological weapon would be an outbreak of disease in humans, animals or plants, considerable attention is being given by the Ad Hoc Group as to how to distinguish a deliberate outbreak (resulting from use of a biological weapon) from a natural outbreak recognising that there is increasing world concern

1

*M. Dando et al. (eds.),*
*Scientific and Technical Means of Distinguishing Between Natural and Other Outbreaks of Disease,* 1–20.
© 2001 *Kluwer Academic Publishers.*

about new, emerging and re-emerging diseases. A leading role is being taken at the Ad Hoc Group by South Africa who were instrumental in proposing[3] that the mandate for the Ad Hoc Group should include consideration of measures to investigate allegations of use. The world concern about disease was evident from the remarks of the Director General of the World Health Organisation (WHO) in the 1996 World Health Report[4] that "We also stand on the brink of a global crisis in infectious diseases. No country is safe from them. No country can any longer afford to ignore their threat."

This introductory chapter sets the scene for the Advanced Research Workshop by considering the background to the investigation of outbreaks of disease, considering why it is necessary to distinguish natural outbreaks from deliberate or accidental outbreaks and examining the mandate and the progress made by the Ad Hoc Group towards a Protocol to strengthen the effectiveness and improve the implementation of the BTWC. It concludes by identifying some of the issues to be addressed by the Workshop.

## 2. Natural and Other Outbreaks of Disease

It is becoming increasingly clear that disease -- in humans, animals or plants -- presents great danger to prosperity and trade. There is increasing international attention being paid to how such outbreaks of disease should be countered with the relevant international organisations -- WHO, OIE and FAO -- taking the lead in strengthening the international provisions for the surveillance and monitoring of outbreaks of disease. This was clearly shown by the adoption by the World Health Assembly in 1995 of a resolution[5] addressing communicable diseases prevention and control: new, emerging and re-emerging infectious diseases. This resolution noted in its preamble: *that more frequent international travel leads to rapid global exchange of human pathogens; that changes in health technology and food production, as well as its distribution (including international trade) and handling, create new opportunities for human pathogens* and goes on to urge Member States inter alia:

> To strengthen national and local programmes of active surveillance for infectious diseases, ensuring that efforts are directed to early detection of outbreaks and prompt identification of new, emerging and re-emerging infectious diseases

> To enhance, and to participate actively in, communications between national and international services involved in disease detection, early notification, surveillance, control and response;

> To control outbreaks and to promote accurate and timely reporting of cases at national and international levels

and requests the WHO to develop strategies and plans enabling rapid national and international action to investigate and combat infectious disease outbreaks and epidemics.

The importance of infectious disease was highlighted by the G8 Summit of Heads of State and Government which at their summit in Denver in 1997 stated that infectious diseases are responsible for a third of all deaths in the world. They pose significant challenges to the health, security and financial resources of the global community. In many parts of the world, infectious diseases and death from infectious disease have risen sharply in the last decade for a variety of reasons, including the emergence of drug-resistant microbes and the increased movement of people and products. It is worth noting the recognition by the G8 of the significant challenges posed by infectious diseases to the **health, security and financial resources of the global community.**

## 3. Deliberate Disease

A deliberate attack using disease as a weapon against humans, animals or plants is biological warfare. President Clinton in his address[6] to the United Nations General Assembly on 24 September 1996 said *"we must better protect our people from those who would use disease as a weapon of war"*. [Emphasis added]. The use of disease as a weapon of war goes back into antiquity[7] and to examples such as the use of smallpox infected blankets in gifts to the American Indians. Biological warfare is included in the Geneva Protocol of 1925 which prohibited the use of chemical or biological materials in war, and, in 1972, the Biological and Toxin Weapons Convention was opened for signature and entered into force in 1975 prohibiting the development, production, stockpiling or acquisition of an entire class of weapons -- biological and toxin weapons. Because biological agents (other than toxins) multiply in the infected target population, the quantities needed to cause infection are very much smaller than the amounts of chemical agent needed to cause harm - a few biological micro-organisms may suffice. Consequently, biological weapons have a significantly larger potential area of effect than have chemical weapons and hence the potential impact of biological weapons approaches that of nuclear weapons and can have strategic effects.

## CBW DOWNWIND HAZARD

| | Classical CW | Industrial Pharmaceutical Chemicals | Bioregulators Peptides | Toxins | Genetically Modified BW | Traditional BW |
|---|---|---|---|---|---|---|
| 1 km | | | | | | |
| 10 km | | | | | | |
| 100km | | | | | | |
| 1000 km | | | | | | |

The downwind hazard can extend to a few hundred kilometres if the meteorological conditions are optimum.   As the quantities required for BW are small compared to chemical weapons, they can be disseminated by cross-wind dissemination with few if any indications of hostile intent.   A simple dissemination system such as one mounted on a single aircraft flying across the wind could be used to produce a line source of 200 km or so long resulting in an attack of an area of some 200 km wide by 200 km downwind; a vehicle driven across the wind could produce a shorter line source of perhaps 50 km in length attacking a proportionately smaller area.   The Office of Technology Assessment of the US Congress in an evaluation[8] of weapons of mass destruction showed that a single aircraft attack of Washington DC using anthrax could result in 1 to 3 million deaths; in the same scenario, a one megaton hydrogen bomb would only cause some 0.5 to 1.9 million deaths.   Such attacks with biological agents present a serious challenge to personnel in military targets such as naval task forces and assembly areas or to strategic targets.   Likewise, if used to attack livestock or plants, a significant effect could be produced.   Although BW were perceived to be unreliable and to offer the prospect of inadvertently attacking one's own forces, the feasibility of BW was demonstrated in UK and US trials prior to the termination of those retaliatory programmes.   There is thus no doubt about the danger posed by such weapons -- and it is for that reason that they are totally prohibited by the BTWC which entered into force in 1975.

A useful comparison (see Table 1) of nuclear, biological and chemical weapons was made by a US Congressional Committee[9] which shows clearly that biological weapons are the easiest to acquire as many pathogens are endemic -- i.e. occur in nature, have the least cost and least signature yet have comparable strategic effects to nuclear weapons. Taken together, it is clear that **biological weapons present the greatest danger today** of all three weapons of mass destruction as they are the easiest to acquire, have the weakest regime and yet have effects comparable to nuclear weapons. Consequently, countering biological weapons is a key security priority.

When the arms control regimes associated with the three types of weapons of mass destruction are considered, it is clear that the Nuclear Non-Proliferation Treaty regime augmented by the '93 + 2' Additional Protocol and the Chemical Weapons Convention (CWC) regime are much stronger than that of the BTWC. Indeed, it is for that reason that the BTWC is the subject of ongoing negotiations of a Protocol to strengthen the BTWC.

TABLE 1

| Type | Technology | Cost | Signature | Effectiveness | |
| | | | | Tactical | Strategic |
| Nuclear | Very high | Very high | Very high | Very high | Very high |
| **Biological** | **High** | **Low** | **Low** | **Low** | **Very high** |
| Chemical | High | High | High | Very high | Low |

It is thus evident that the cost and signature associated with a biological weapons programme is less than that associated with chemical or nuclear weapons, and because the prohibition regime is currently the weakest, biological weapons today pose the greatest danger.

So what has happened over the past two decades to cause President Clinton to express his concern to the United Nations? The past two decades has seen the burgeoning of biotechnology making it easier to produce biological materials and to modify them so as to enhance their effects. Advances in microbiology, genetic engineering and biotechnology have seen immense benefits for the health of people and animals around the world with the biotechnology industry being one of the principal growth areas offering the prospect of new and improved diagnostic techniques and medical countermeasures to the increasing range of diseases that threaten the health and well-being of people and animals worldwide. However, the diseases which these advances are used to counter occur in nature and the counters require an understanding of the ways in which such diseases attack the target population - and therein lies the difficulty of enforcing the Biological and Toxin Weapons Convention (BTWC) as both the causative agents and the methods used to produce them are **dual purpose** and can be used **both** for prohibited purposes as well as for permitted purposes to promote health and well-being.

Although the BTWC totally prohibits the development, production, acquisition or storage of biological weapons, it does not specifically address the prohibition of use. However, the Preamble in stating that *Determined, for the sake of all mankind, to exclude completely the possibility of bacteriological(biological) agents and toxins being used as weapons*, makes it clear that the intent is to prohibit use. This intent to prohibit use was reinforced at the Fourth Review Conference[10] by language stating that:

> *The Conference reaffirms that **the use by the States Parties, in any way and under any circumstances,** of microbial or other biological agents or toxins, that is not consistent with prophylactic, protective or other peaceful purposes, is effectively a violation of Article I of the Convention.*

> *The Conference reaffirms the undertaking in Article I never in any circumstance to develop, produce, stockpile or otherwise acquire or retain weapons, equipment or means of delivery designed to use such agents or toxins for hostile purposes or in armed conflict, **in order to exclude completely and forever the possibility of their use.***[Emphasis added]

### 4. Unusual Outbreaks

It has long been recognised that an unusual outbreak may be the first indication of the use of a biological weapon. This was recognised by the States Parties to the BTWC at the Second Review Conference in 1986 which agreed[11] that *the States Parties are to implement, on the basis of mutual cooperation, the following measures, in order to prevent or reduce the occurrence of ambiguities, doubts and suspicions, and in order to improve international cooperation in the field of peaceful bacteriological (biological activities): ...*

> 2. Exchange of information on all outbreaks of infectious diseases and similar occurrences caused by toxins that seem to deviate from the normal pattern as regards type, development, place, or time of occurrence. If possible the information provided would include, as soon as it is available, data on the type of disease, approximate area affected, and number of cases.

At the subsequent Ad Hoc meeting[12] held on 31 March to 15 April 1997, the States Parties considered the modalities for this confidence-building measure (CBM) and the Ad Hoc meeting agreed on the following:

1. In determining what constitutes an outbreak States Parties are recommended to take guidance from the above [definitions of an outbreak from the WHO and from the *Dictionary of Epidemiology*]

2. Since no universal standards exist for what might constitute a deviation from the normal pattern, States Parties are encouraged

- to fully utilise existing reporting systems within the WHO, and

- provide background information on diseases caused by organisms which meet the criteria for risk groups III and IV according to the classification in the 1983 WHO *Laboratory Biosafety Manual*, the occurrence of which, in their respective areas, does not necessarily constitute a deviation from normal patterns.

3. The exchange of data on outbreaks which seem to deviate from the normal pattern is considered particularly important in the following cases:

- when the cause of the outbreak cannot be readily determined or the causative agent* is difficult to diagnose,

[* It is understood that this may include organisms made pathogenic by molecular biology techniques]

- when the disease may be caused by organisms which meet the criteria for risk groups III and IV according to the classification in the 1983 WHO Laboratory Biosafety Manual,

- when the causative agent is exotic to a given region,

- when the disease follows an unusual pattern of development,

- when the disease occurs in the vicinity of research centres and laboratories subject to exchange of data under item A.

- when suspicions arise of the possible occurrence of a new disease.

At the subsequent Third Review Conference in 1991, the States Parties in their Final Declaration[13] agreed the modalities agreed at the Ad Hoc meeting in 1987. They extended the language in paragraph 2 to include both animal and plant diseases as follows:

> 2. Since no universal standards exist for what might constitute a deviation from the normal pattern, States Parties **agreed** to utilise **fully** existing **national** reporting systems **on human diseases as well as animal and plant diseases, where possible, and systems** within the WHO to provide **annual update of** background information on diseases caused by organisms which meet the criteria for risk groups II, III and IV according to the classification in the 1983 WHO *Laboratory Biosafety Manual*, the occurrence of which, in their respective areas, does not necessarily constitute a deviation from normal patterns. [The emphasis in bold shows the modified language agreed in 1991].

It is, however, unfortunate that the annual declarations made under this CBM have been variable and patchy. Consequently, an analysis of these declarations cannot be used to draw up a set of criteria characteristic of an unusual outbreak.

## 5. Outbreaks of Disease

It is thus evident that there are a number of questions that need to be asked about any outbreak of disease:

* What are its characteristics?
* Where did outbreak originate?
* How to contain & counter the outbreak?
* How to prevent recurrence?

It is only then possible to ask the question as to whether it was a natural or other outbreak? In so doing, it was important to bear in mind that other outbreaks could result from accidental release. If an outbreak appeared to result from causes other than those occurring in nature, then it was necessary to consider who the perpetrator might have been and what action might be taken to counter further outbreaks and to ensure no recurrence. The importance of being able to distinguish between natural and other causes was thus evident.

## 6. The Biological and Toxin Weapons Convention (BTWC)

As already noted, this totally prohibits the development, production, acquisition and storage of biological weapons and their use is prohibited implicitly through the Preamble and explicitly through the Final Declaration of the Fourth Review Conference. The BTWC was agreed at a time when treaties were generally short documents - the BTWC is some four pages long - and contained no provisions for verification. The past 20 years has seen the acceptance internationally of on-site inspection in all recent arms control treaties - the Chemical Weapons Convention has a detailed Verification Annex of some 100 pages which details how on-site inspections including investigations of alleged use may be carried out making it clear that the onus is on the Inspected State to demonstrate to the Inspectorate that it is in compliance with the Convention.     In parallel with the increased acceptance of on-site inspection in arms control treaties, it has become apparent that biological weapons have become an attractive option for a number of States and their proliferation has increased during the past 20 years.

This concern about non-compliance with the BTWC has been sharpened during the past decade first by the admission by President Yeltsin in 1992 that the former Soviet Union, despite being a codepositary along with the United Kingdom and the United States of the BTWC, had continued an offensive biological weapons programme in breach of the Convention for 20 years up to 1992. Then in 1995, Iraq disclosed to the United Nations Special Commission (UNSCOM) that, despite being a signatory of the BTWC, Iraq had had a significant biological weapons programme which had seen the filling of aerial bombs and of Al Hussein missile warheads with biological agents and their deployment to four locations in the run up to the Gulf War of 1991. It has also become apparent with the use of the nerve agent sarin in the attacks in the Tokyo subway in March 1995 by the Aum Shinrikyo sect and their interest in acquiring biological weapons that there is a real danger that chemical and biological materials may be used for terrorist purposes - and this led the Heads of the G7 States at their meeting in Lyon, France on 27 June 1996 in their Declaration on Terrorism to state[14] that "Special attention should be paid to the **threat of utilisation of** nuclear, **biological** and chemical **materials**, as well as toxic substances, **for terrorist purposes.**" [Emphasis added]

The past decade has seen a move from the bipolar super–power stand–off of the Cold War era into a rash of regional conflicts around the world and collapsed economies. The deliberate use of disease – against humans, animals or plants – may become to be regarded as a possible option, if we do not take action to make this unattractive, especially by small States whose conventional military capabilities may be limited. The window of opportunity to do this is now through the negotiation of a Protocol to strengthen the BTWC thereby bringing benefits not only for national, regional and international security but also for national and international prosperity and trade.

At the Third Review Conference, the States Parties agreed to establish an Ad Hoc Group of Governmental Experts *to identify and examine potential verification measures from a scientific and technical standpoint.* The report of this group, known as VEREX, was considered by a Special Conference in 1994 which agreed[15] to establish an Ad Hoc Group *to consider appropriate measures, including possible verification measures, ... to be included, as appropriate, in a legally binding instrument.* The Final Declaration of the Special Conference also included the requirement that *This regime would include, inter alia, potential verification measures and mechanisms for their efficient implementation and measures for the investigation of alleged use.* [Emphasis added].

The Ad Hoc Group held its first meeting in January 1995 and had in July 1997 made a successful transition to consideration of the rolling text of a draft Protocol. By October

1998, this had reached its sixth version[16] which contained all the essential elements for a Protocol. The Ad Hoc Group negotiations have been progressed by a appointment of a number of Friends of the Chair who chair the meetings relating to particular elements of the Protocol. In October 1998, the Friends of the Chair of particular relevance to investigations of unusual outbreaks were:

- Compliance Measures      Richard Tauwhare, UK
- Investigations Annex      Peter Goosen, South Africa
- Article X measures      Carlos Duarte, Brazil
- Organization      Tibor Toth, Hungary
- Confidence Building Measures      Tibor Toth, Hungary

The October 1998 draft Protocol contains provisions for the following:

*Declarations of most relevant facilities
*Declaration follow up procedures including infrequent visits to declared facilities
*Declaration clarification procedures to address ambiguities, uncertainties, anomalies and omissions including visits
* Investigations of compliance concerns -- both facility and **field**
* An Organization to implement Protocol
* Measures to implement Article X of BTWC

There was a useful indication in July 1998 of the progress being made towards consensus in respect of the Protocol by the presentation of a Working Paper 296[17] by 29 States Parties which noted that the draft protocol included provisions for:

- Declarations of a range of facilities and activities of potential relevance
- Provision for visits to facilities in order to promote accurate and complete declarations
- Provisions for rapid and effective investigations into concerns over non-compliance
- A cost-effective and independent Organization

- ...above States Parties reaffirm their commitment to actively promote and engage in international cooperation and exchanges in biotechnology....Further they look forward to the development of specific measures in Article VII of the Protocol....Such measures should also address needs for assistance to ensure the Protocol's implementation.

- ...intensifying its efforts towards the successful and early adoption of a legally-binding Protocol

In considering the draft Protocol text, it is important to recognise that:

* The complete text is **not** reviewed at each meeting
* However, a complete text is attached to each procedural report which contains the latest text
    - outcome of negotiations is incorporated
    - unreviewed text is reproduced unchanged

In addition, papers are also prepared and attached to Part II of the procedural report by the Friends of the Chair for consideration by the Ad Hoc Group in which clean text is produced containing proposals to remove the square brackets indicating alternative language. This clean text provides an indication of the way in which the Friends of the Chair envisage the Protocol text developing towards the final version.

## 7. Outbreaks of Disease in the Draft Protocol

There are several places in the October 1998 draft Protocol where reference is made to outbreaks of disease. These are the following:

* Art III Compliance Measures
    - **Investigation of alleged use**
* Art VII Technical Cooperation
    - **Global monitoring of disease**
* Art IX Organization
    - **Co-operative arrangements**
* Annex D - Investigations - **alleged use**
* Annex G - CBM IV Multilateral Information Sharing
    - **Surveillance of disease outbreaks**

In *Article III Compliance Measures F. [Visits and Investigations] III. Investigations* there is language regarding the initiation and types of investigations which includes the following:

4. The requesting State Party [the State Party requesting an investigation (hereinafter referred to as the "Requesting State Party")] shall specify in each request which one of the following types of investigation it is seeking:

1) [Field] investigations [of the alleged use of biological weapons] [, to be conducted in geographic areas where the release of, or exposure of humans, animals or plants to microbial or other biological agents and/or toxins has given rise to a concern about non-compliance with Article I of the Convention by a State Party].

(2) [Facility] investigations [of any other alleged breach of obligations under the provisions of the Convention] [, to be conducted inside the perimeter of a particular facility(ies) for which there is a concern that it is involved in activities prohibited by Article I of the Convention].

These two categories of investigation are referred to as "field" and "facility" investigations respectively. Clearly, "field" investigations are those primarily associated with unusual outbreaks of disease.

The draft Protocol then includes language resulting from the argument put forward by the NAM (Non-Aligned Movement) and Other States in WP.262[18] which states that *"All natural outbreaks of disease fall in the domain of public health and do not pose a compliance concern to the Biological and Toxin Weapons Convention (BTWC), and therefore are of no concern to the Convention or to its proposed Protocol."* and seeks to ensure that an outbreak of disease **by itself** is not a justification for the mounting of an investigation under the Protocol. In October 1998, there were three versions of this paragraph, the first of which 5. was proposed in WP.262:

5. All natural outbreaks of disease do not pose a compliance concern to the Convention [and therefore shall not be cause for an investigation of a non-compliance concern] [as set out in Annex ...].

[5 bis All natural outbreaks of disease do not pose a compliance concern to the Convention and therefore shall not be a cause for an investigation of a non-compliance concern. The diseases which are endemic in the region and present the expected epidemiological features shall not be considered as a unusual outbreak of disease. An outbreak of disease which appears to be unusual, shall be investigated by the affected State Party, as per guidelines set out in Annex D, section V, and concluded as soon as possible.]

[5 ter Accidents which are a result of activities not prohibited under the Convention do not pose a compliance concern to the Convention and therefore shall not be cause for an investigation of a non-compliance concern as set out in Annex ... .]

This shows the tension amongst the States Parties between those who see investigation of an alleged use as being a key element of the Protocol and those who are concerned that an outbreak of disease might be regarded as justification for an mounting an investigation under the Protocol. WP.262 put forward some reasons why an outbreak may be unusual and unexpected:

Unusual outbreak of disease could have natural causes despite their unusual characteristics. On the other hand, it is possible to visualise a situation when the outbreak of certain diseases with atypical characteristics may be viewed as the result of possible "use" of Biological and Toxin Weapons. It, therefore, becomes essential to develop guidelines to differentiate between the two. It is of the utmost importance to differentiate natural outbreaks of disease and an event of non-compliance with BTW Convention.

An unusual outbreak of disease may be defined as an outbreak which is unexpected within the prevailing context for the host agent and environment parameters. It may be unusual and also unexpected because of one or more of the following reasons:

(a) The disease is being reported for the first time in the region and was never endemic;

(b) The epidemic occurs outside its normal anticipated season;

(c) The reservoir host and/or insect vector of the disease do not occur in or were previously eradicated from the affected region;

(d) The disease appears to be transmitted by an uncommon or unusual route;

(e) The epidemiological features of the disease suggest increased virulence of the organism manifested in the form of increased case fatality rate;

(f) The causative agent has higher survival time even in the adverse environmental conditions and shows unusual resistance;

(g) Is capable of establishing new natural reservoirs to facilitate continuous transmission;

(h) Outbreaks of the disease in a population with a high level of immunity due to vaccination suggesting that the causative agent is modified;

(i) The disease is caused by an agent with an unusual population subset or in an unexpected age group;

(j) The epidemiology of the disease suggests an abnormal reduction in the incubation period of the disease;

(k) When the epidemiology of the outbreak strongly points to an etiology, but isolation and identification of the suspected agent is not possible by established means;

(i) When the characteristics of the causative agent differ from the known characteristics of that agent prevalent in the territory of the State Party.

The draft Protocol in October 1998 in *Article III. F. III Investigations* contained language concerning the information to be submitted with requests for field investigations as follows:

16. Requests for [field] investigations [into alleged use of biological weapons] under paragraph 4 of this Article for an event(s) which has

14

given rise to a concern about non-compliance shall at least include the following information:

(a) Name of the State [Party] on whose territory or in any other place under whose jurisdiction or control the alleged event(s) has taken place;

(b) If the alleged event(s) has taken place, in any place on the territory of a State [Party] which is not under its jurisdiction or control, the name of that State [Party] [(hereinafter referred to as the "host State Party/State")];

(c) A description of the event(s), including all [available] information on:

(i) The [use] [release] of microbial or other biological agent(s) or toxin(s) for other than peaceful purposes; and/or

(ii) Weapons, equipment or means of delivery used in the alleged event(s);

(d) The circumstances under which the event(s) took place;

(e) The suspected cause and/or perpetrator of the event(s);

(f) The date and time when the alleged event(s) took place and [/or] became apparent to the requesting State Party and, if possible, the duration of that event(s);

(g) The area requested to be investigated identified as precisely as possible by providing the geographic co-ordinates, specified to the nearest second if possible, or other alternative measures, as well as a map specifying the identified area and the geographic characteristics of the area;

(h) Whether the victims are humans, animals or plants as well as an indication of numbers affected and a description of the consequences of exposure;

(i) Symptoms and/or signs of the disease;

(j) All available epidemiological data relevant to the disease outbreak;

[(k) Substantiating evidence to differentiate the event(s) to be investigated from a natural outbreak of disease and demonstrate that it is not a natural outbreak of disease [or accidents which are a result of activities not prohibited under the Convention];]

[(l) Information from and/or the outcome or results of [any] prior consultations/ clarifications relevant to the request.]

17. In addition to the information to be supplied with a request pursuant to paragraph 16, other types of information may also be submitted as appropriate and to the extent possible including, inter alia:

(a) Reports of any internal investigation including results of any laboratory investigations;

(b) Information on the initial treatment and the preliminary results of the treatment of the disease;

(c) A description of the measures taken to prevent the spread of the disease outbreak and to eliminate the consequences of the event(s), and their results in the affected area, if available;

(d) [Request for specific assistance] [Information on any requests for assistance relevant to the alleged event(s)], if applicable;

[(e) In the case of alleged accidental release of microbial or other biological agents or toxins, information on a facility(ies) from which the accidental release could have taken place;]

(f) Any other corroborative information, including affidavits of eye witness accounts, photographs, samples or other physical evidence [which in the course of internal investigations have been recognised as being related to the event(s)].

A further paragraph, albeit within square brackets, seeks the provision of information indicating that the outbreak is potentially connected to activities prohibited by the BTWC:

[18. To avoid abusive or frivolous requests, in addition to the requirements set forth in paragraph 16, requests for a field investigation based upon an outbreak of disease or intoxification of concern shall contain information indicating that such outbreak is potentially connected to activities prohibited by the Convention. The State Party on whose territory the field investigation is proposed to occur or any other State Party may provide any information that indicates such outbreak of disease or intoxification is naturally occurring or otherwise unrelated to activities prohibited by the Convention. This information shall also be taken into account by the [Executive] [Consultative] Council in its consideration of the investigation request in accordance with the request procedures of paragraph ... of this Article.]

Elsewhere in the October 1998 version of the Protocol there are other provisions relating to the outbreaks of disease. For example, in *Article VII [Scientific and Technical Exchange for Peaceful Purposes] [Implementation Assistance] and Technical Cooperation* there is language for measures to promote scientific and technical exchanges which includes:

(d) Promote public health, as well as the monitoring, diagnosis, prevention and control of outbreaks of diseases...

[(f) Assist in improving and participating in the functioning of international systems for the global monitoring of emerging diseases in humans, animals or plants;]

There is also language in *Annex G Confidence-Building Measures* under *IV. Multilateral Information Sharing* which includes detail under the following headings:

3.3 Surveillance of disease outbreaks and unusual disease outbreak reports

3.3.1 Surveillance of human disease outbreak and unusual disease outbreak reports

3.3.2 Surveillance of animal disease outbreak reports

3.3.3 Surveillance of plant disease outbreak reports

Throughout the October 1998 version of the Protocol there are various references, generally within square brackets to the possible involvement of the WHO/IOE/FAO in relation to outbreaks of disease. For example, in the context of Consultation, Clarification and Cooperation within Article III. F. III. Investigations there is language that:

[[International organisations such as WHO, FAO and OIE][and an international epidemiological network] may play a role in such consultation and clarification procedures.]

and later in the same Article in the context of Follow-up After Submission of an Investigation Request there is heavily bracketed language that:

[The [Executive] [Consultative] Council may also consider whether to request more information from [other relevant international organisations] [such as] [WHO/IOE/FAO] [that would be necessary for taking a decision on a request] [which it considers necessary for further consideration of the investigation request] [or whether to request the WHO/IOE/FAO to conduct an investigation].]]]

It is, however, clear elsewhere in the October 1998 version of the Protocol, notably in Annex D Investigations, in unbracketed language that the intention is that investigations shall be carried out by the BTWC Protocol Organisation.

## 8. Advanced Research Workshop Structure

The Workshop has been structured so as to start by focussing on the importance of distinguishing between natural and other outbreaks of disease, then considering the diseases of concern and what mechanisms exist for identifying outbreaks. Consideration is then given to the scientific characteristics of natural outbreaks before addressing the technical characteristics of a BW attack whether against humans, animals or plants and how such attacks might differ from a natural outbreak. A further series of presentations then considers the scientific techniques available for investigating an outbreak and to what extent such techniques can indicate whether an outbreak has resulted from a natural or other cause. The information that has become available from an accidental release at Sverdlovsk is examined to see what lessons this can provide for investigations of alleged use. Consideration is then given to the strengths and weaknesses of disease surveillance and to technical contributions to countering outbreaks. Finally, a round table discussion will draw together the principal conclusions from the workshop in regard to scientific and technological methods of distinguishing between biological weapons attacks and natural disease outbreaks.

Some of the issues to be discussed during the Workshop include the following:

* There is no definition in Protocol of "natural outbreak" for what appear to be sound reasons.

* Are not all outbreaks "natural" in that their characteristics once initiated are the same whether resulting from natural or other causes?

* How realistic is it in the Protocol to propose language that *All natural outbreaks of disease do not pose a compliance concern to the Convention [and therefore shall not be cause for an investigation of a non-compliance concern]...*

* How can natural and other outbreaks be distinguished
         - epidemiologically?
         - analytical techniques?
         - any other techniques?

* What should be the relationship between the WHO and the future BTWC Protocol Organization
         - WHO primary role must be protected
         - BTWCO needs to monitor outbreaks of disease

* The idea that the WHO might conduct verification activities for the BTWC Protocol Organization appears incompatible with the primary function of the WHO

18

* How will investigations be initiated?
> - The Protocol proposes that the State Party will request investigation (not the BTWC Protocol Organization)

* The BTWC Protocol Organization will need to be professionally competent in epidemiology

**Notes**

[1]United Nations, *Convention on the Prohibition of the Development, Production and Stockpiling of Bacteriological (Biological) and Toxin Weapons and on their Destruction*, General Assembly resolution 2826(XXVI), 16 December 1971.

[2]NATO, *Madrid Declaration on Euro-Atlantic Security and Cooperation Issued by the Heads of State and Government*, Press Release, M - 1 (97) 81, Meeting of the North Atlantic Council, Madrid, 8 July 1997. Available at http://www.nato.int/docu/pr/1997/p97-18e.htm

[3]South Africa, *Mandate to Strengthen the Biological and Toxin Weapons Convention*, Working Paper 11, BWC/SPCONF/1, Part III, page 38, Geneva, 19 - 30 September 1994.

[4]World Health Organisation, *World Health Report 1996, Fighting disease, Fostering development"*, ISBN 92 4 156182 3, Geneva, 1996.

[5]World Health Assembly, Resolution WHA48.13, *Communicable Diseases Prevention And Control: New, Emerging and Re-Emerging Infectious Diseases*, 12 May 1995. Available at http://www.who.int

[6]The White House, *Remarks by the President in Address to the 51st General Assembly of the United Nations*, 24 September 1996.

[7]Mark Wheelis, *Biological warfare before 1914*, in *Biological and Toxin Weapons: Research, Development and Use from the Middle Ages to 1945*, ed. Erhard Geissler and John Ellis van Courtland Moon, SIPRI, Oxford University Press, 1999.

[8]United States Congress, Office of Technology Assessment, *Proliferation of Weapons of Mass Destruction: Assessing the Risks*, OTA-ISC-559, S/N 052-003-01335-5, dated 5 August 1993. United States Congress, Office of Technology Assessment, Background Paper, *Technologies Underlying Weapons of Mass Destruction*, OTA-BP-ISC-115, S/N 052-003-01361-4, dated December 1993.

[9]US Congress, Committee on Armed Services, House of Representatives, 23 February 1993.

[10]United Nations, *Fourth Review Conference of the Parties to the Convention on the Prohibition of the Development, Production and Stockpiling of Bacteriological (Biological) and Toxin Weapons and on their Destruction, Final Declaration*, Final Document, BWC/CONF.IV/9, 6 December 1996.

[11]United Nations, *The Second Review Conference of the States Parties to the Convention on the Prohibition of the Development, Production and Stockpiling of Bacteriological (Biological) and Toxin Weapons and on their Destruction, Final Declaration*, Final Document, Geneva, 8–26 September 1986, BWC/CONF.II/13, Geneva 1986.

[12]United Nations, *Ad Hoc Meeting of Scientific and Technical Experts from States Parties to the Convention on the Prohibition of the Development, Production and Stockpiling of Bacteriological (Biological) and Toxin Weapons and on their Destruction*, BWC/CONF.II/EX/2, 21 April 1987.

[13]United Nations, *The Third Review Conference of the States Parties to the Convention on the Prohibition of the Development, Production and Stockpiling of Bacteriological (Biological and Toxin Weapons and on their Destruction, Final Declaration*, Final Document, Geneva 9–27 September 1991, BWC/CONF.III/23, Geneva 1992.

[14]United Nations General Assembly/Security Council, *Letter dated 5 July 1996 from the Permanent Representative of France to the United Nations addressed to the Secretary-General*, A/51/208, S/1996/543, 12 July 1996. Annex V: Declaration on Terrorism, Lyon, 27 June 1996.

[15]United Nations, *Special Conference of the Parties to the Convention on the Prohibition of the Development, Production and Stockpiling of Bacteriological (Biological) and Toxin Weapons and on their Destruction*, Geneva, 19 - 30 September 1994, Final Report, BWC/SPCONF/1, 1994.

[16]United Nations, *Ad Hoc Group of the Parties to the Convention on the Prohibition of the Development, Production and Stockpiling of Bacteriological (Biological) and Toxin Weapons and on their Destruction*, BWC/AD HOC GROUP/43 (Part I), 15 October 1998.

[17]Argentina, Australia, Austria, Belgium, Bulgaria, Canada, Czech Republic, Denmark, Finland, France, Germany, Greece, Ireland, Italy, Japan, Netherlands, New Zealand, Norway, Poland, Portugal, Republic of Korea, Romania, Slovakia, Spain, Sweden, Switzerland, Turkey, United Kingdom and the United States, BWC/AD HOC GROUP/WP.296, 10 July 1998.

[18]Group of NAM and Other Countries, *Investigations: Exclusion of All Natural Outbreaks of Disease*, BWC/ AD HOC GROUP/WP.262, 23 January 1998.

# OUTBREAKS OF DISEASE

AMBASSADOR TIBOR TÓTH
*Permanent Representative of Hungary
to the United Nations Office in Vienna*

## 1. Introduction

In considering outbreaks of disease, there are four key issues which need to be addressed:

* Non-use regimes dealing with outbreaks of disease
* The reporting mechanisms for disease outbreaks and trends
* Challenges facing the Ad Hoc Group in addressing outbreaks of disease
* Possible solutions for the Ad Hoc Group

Each of these is considered in turn.

## 2. Non-Use Regimes for Outbreaks of Disease

There are two elements in such regimes -- those concerned with prohibition and those concerned with investigation.

### 2.1 PROHIBITION ELEMENTS

The prohibition elements consist of the following main building blocks:

### 2.1.1 1925 *Geneva Protocol.*

This Protocol for the Prohibition of the Use in War of Asphyxiating, Poisonous or Other Gases, and Bacteriological Methods of Warfare states that:

> *The Undersigned Plenipotentiaries, in the name of their respective Governments:*
>
> *Whereas the use in war of asphyxiating, poisonous or other gases, and of all analogous liquids, materials or devices, has been justly condemned by the general opinion of the civilised world; ...*

21

M. Dando et al. (eds.),
*Scientific and Technical Means of Distinguishing Between Natural and Other Outbreaks of Disease*, 21–29.
© 2001 *Kluwer Academic Publishers.*

*Declare:*

*That the High Contracting Parties, so far as they are not already Parties to Treaties prohibiting such use, accept this prohibition, agree to extend this prohibition to the use of bacteriological methods of warfare and agree to be bound as between themselves according to the terms of this declaration.*

In acceding to the Geneva Protocol, a number of the States Parties entered reservations to the effect that they would no longer be bound by the Geneva Protocol were such weapons to be used against them by another State. These reservations essentially made the Geneva Protocol a prohibition of the first use of chemical or biological weapons for a number of States. Recently, a number of these reservations have been lifted as the Biological and Toxins Weapons Convention and the Chemical Weapons Convention have come into force.

### 2.1.2 *Biological and Toxin Weapons Convention (BTWC).*

The BTWC opened for signature on 10 April 1972 and entered into force on 26 March 1975 totally prohibits the development, production, acquisition or storage of biological and toxin weapons through the undertaking in Article I:

*Each State Party to this Convention undertakes never in any circumstances to develop, produce, stockpile or otherwise acquire or retain:*

*(1) Microbial or other biological agents, or toxins whatever their origin or method of production, of types and in quantities that have no justification for prophylactic, protective or other peaceful purposes;*

*(2) Weapons, equipment or means of delivery designed to use such agents or toxins for hostile purposes or in armed conflict.*

The BTWC does not specifically address the prohibition of use. However, the Preamble in stating that "Determined, for the sake of all mankind, to exclude completely the possibility of bacteriological(biological) agents and toxins being used as weapons", makes it clear that the intent is to prohibit use.

### 2.1.3 *Chemical Weapons Convention (CWC).*

The CWC opened for signature on 13 - 15 January 1993 and entered into force on 29 April 1997. This totally prohibits the development, production, acquisition, storage or use of chemical weapons through the undertaking in Article I:

1.      *Each State Party to this Convention undertakes never under any circumstances:*

> *(a) To develop, produce, otherwise acquire, stockpile or retain chemical weapons, or transfer, directly or indirectly, chemical weapons to anyone;*

> *(b) To use chemical weapons;*

> *(c) To engage in any military preparations to use chemical weapons;*

> *(d) To assist, encourage or induce, in any way, anyone to engage in any activity prohibited to a State Party under this Convention.*

The prohibition of use is explicitly addressed in the CWC.

### 2.1.4 *Review Conferences of the BTWC.*

At the Review Conferences of the BTWC held at about five year intervals the States Parties have reviewed progress and have agreed Final Declarations which have served to extend understandings between the States Parties. At the Fourth Review Conference in November/December 1996, considerable attention was given to the issue of use. The intent to prohibit use was emphasised by language in the Final Declaration stating that:

> *The Conference reaffirms that **the use by the States Parties, in any way and under any circumstances,** of microbial or other biological agents or toxins, that is not consistent with prophylactic, protective or other peaceful purposes, is effectively a violation of Article I of the Convention.*

> *The Conference reaffirms the undertaking in Article I never in any circumstance to develop, produce, stockpile or otherwise acquire or retain weapons, equipment or means of delivery designed to use such agents or toxins for hostile purposes or in armed conflict, **in order to exclude completely and forever the possibility of their use.***[Emphasis added]

### 2.2 INVESTIGATION ELEMENTS

The investigation elements consist of the following.

### 2.2.1 *1925 Geneva Protocol -- UN Secretary-General's Investigation Mechanisms.*

Although there is no provision in the Geneva Protocol for any investigation of an alleged use of chemical or biological weapons, there have during the past couple of decades been occasions when the United Nations Secretary-General, at the invitation of the State on whose territory the alleged incident has occurred, has dispatched small teams of international experts to investigate the alleged use of chemical weapons. There were several such investigations during the Iran/Iraq war of the 1980s. In general these were carried out using ad hoc procedures which have been used within the constraints of the particular circumstances of the incident and have depended entirely upon the support of the inviting State. The outcome of such investigations have consequently frequently been somewhat ambiguous because of the particular circumstances pertaining to the incident being investigated.

Allegations of the continued use of chemical weapons in the Iraq/Iran war and concern expressed by the United Nations General Assembly over the threat posed to international peace and security by the risk of the use of chemical weapons led the General Assembly on 30 November 1987 to adopt resolution 42/37 C which:

> *Requests the Secretary-General to carry out investigations in response to reports that may be brought to his attention by any Member State concerning the possible use of chemical and bacteriological (biological) or toxin weapons that may constitute a violation of the 1925 Geneva Protocol or other relevant rules of customary international law in order to ascertain the facts of the matter, and to report promptly the results of any such investigation to all Member States;*

In addition, the resolution:

> *Requests the Secretary-General, with the assistance of qualified experts provided by interested Member States, to develop further technical guidelines and procedures available to him for the timely and efficient investigation of such reports of the possible use of chemical and bacteriological (biological) or toxin weapons;*

The Secretary-General appointed a group of six qualified experts from Bulgaria, Egypt, France, the Soviet Union, Sweden and the United States which met in Geneva first from 15 to 18 August 1988 and then again from 6 to 17 February 1989 and 31 July to 11 August 1989. The report of the qualified experts to the Secretary-General was circulated by the Secretary-General to the General Assembly as document A/44/561 on 4 October 1989. In this document, the Secretary-General in paragraph 7 noted that the recommendations contained in the report are those of the experts themselves and that the Secretary-General wished *"to point out that, with respect to the complex and technical issues covered by the report, he is not in a position to pass judgement on all aspects of the work accomplished out by the experts."*

Investigations carried out at the request of the UN Secretary General are entirely dependent on an invitation from the State on whose territory the alleged incident has taken place and on whatever access that State decides to provide to the team of experts.

*2.2.2 Chemical Weapons Convention (CWC) -- Challenge Inspections.*

The CWC includes provisions for the carrying out of challenge inspections to address concerns about possible non-compliance with the Convention by a State Party. These provisions include challenge inspections in the case of alleged use; the procedures to be followed are elaborated in *Part XI Investigations in Cases of Alleged Use of Chemical Weapons* of the Verification Annex to the CWC.

*2.2.3 Biological and Toxin Weapons Convention (BTWC) and Review Conferences.*

The BTWC contains no specific provisions for the investigation of an alleged use of biological or toxin weapons. However, Article VI of the Convention makes provision for the lodging of a complaint regarding non-compliance with the Convention with the Security Council of the United Nations:

> *(1) Any State Party to this convention which finds that any other State Party is acting in breach of obligations deriving from the provisions of the Convention may lodge a complaint with the Security Council of the United Nations. Such a complaint should include all possible evidence confirming its validity, as well as a request for its consideration by the Security Council.*

> *(2) Each State Party to this Convention undertakes to cooperate in carrying out any investigation which the Security Council may initiate, in accordance with the provisions of the Charter of the United Nations, on the basis of the complaint received by the Council. The Security Council shall inform the States Parties to the Convention of the results of the investigation.*

Article V of the BTWC provides for States Parties to consult and cooperate in solving any problems:

> *The States Parties to this Convention undertake to consult one another and to cooperate in solving any problems which may arise in relation to the objective of, or in the application of the provisions of, the Convention. Consultation and Cooperation pursuant to this article may also be undertaken through appropriate international procedures within the framework of the United Nations and in accordance with its Charter.*

A procedure for such consultation and cooperation has been elaborated by the BTWC Review Conferences. In 1997 this consultative procedure was invoked at the request of

Cuba in relation to a concern relating to an infestation of *Thrips palmi* on the island of Cuba.

It is therefore apparent that in 1998 there are some deficiencies in respect of outbreaks of disease which may have resulted from the use of biological or toxin weapons. A legally binding CWC investigation can be related only to toxins, the UN Secretary-General investigations related to the 1925 Geneva Protocol are not legally binding and are virtually untested, and the BTWC consultation/investigation process is underdeveloped whilst the UN Security Council is politically too heavy to be invoked. There is, thus, a clear requirement for the Protocol to the BTWC to include measures to enable the investigation of an alleged use of biological or toxin weapons.

### 3. Outbreak Reporting and Investigation Trends

There are currently three reporting mechanisms of particular relevance:

> * BTWC Confidence Building Measures
> * WHO International Health Regulations reports
> * FAO & OIE reports

There are reporting inadequacies for each of these. Although the requirement under the BTWC Confidence Building Measure B agreed at the Second Review Conference for:

> *2. Exchange of information on all outbreaks of infectious diseases and similar occurrences caused by toxins that seem to deviate from the normal pattern as regards type, development, place, or time of occurrence. If possible the information provided would include, as soon as it is available, data on the type of disease, approximate area affected, and number of cases.*

is politically binding, such reports as have been provided have been either incomplete or no reports have been provided; in any event, the data provided in the CBMs is simply collated by the UN Centre for Disarmament Affairs and is not analysed or processed.

The WHO International Health Regulations (IHR) require reports on only three diseases and are not obligatory in a legal sense so they might be regarded as similar to the CBMs. The FAO and OIE reports have long lead times and specificity problems.

Insofar as outbreak surveillance is concerned, there are further inadequacies. There is no mechanism for surveillance under the BTWC CBMs whilst in respect of the WHO, a WHO investigation can only be made at the invitation of the country within which the outbreak had occurred and such an investigation would be limited to the WHO mandate. It would not be possible to extend the scope of a WHO investigation to address other aspects, such as compliance with the BTWC, as the WHO could not jeopardize its primary role of health care.

The trends in outbreak reporting in respect of the WHO is towards a revised IHR which would be based on syndrome-based reporting. This is currently being developed and is the subject of a trial. The adoption of revised IHR will eventually be considered by the World Health Assembly. In addition, there are moves by the WHO/FAO/OIE towards integrated reporting -- the idea of one-stop shopping in reporting outbreak data. There are already yearly reports on disease outbreaks and further efforts are being made towards more holistic reporting. Efforts are also being made by the WHO and NGOs to strengthen the global and regional surveillance networks. A key question is how much money might be made available for such improvements.

### 4. Ad Hoc Group – Challenges

In the context of the Ad Hoc Group negotiations, it is evident that information about outbreaks of disease is clearly relevant to considerations of field investigations. However, there are a number of challenges that the Ad Hoc Group would need to address:

> **a. Public Health.** Outbreaks of disease are frequently unusual yet result from natural causes and would not, of itself, be a concern to the BTWC. This is a particular NAM concern.

> **b. Political Issues.** Some States are concerned about accidental releases and whether or not these might be the subject of a field investigation.

> **c. Mandate.** The mandates of the Ad Hoc Group and the WHO are quite different yet there is a potential synergy. Attention needs to be given to how to access this synergy.

> **d. Coverage.** Reporting to the WHO, FAO and OIE does not necessarily cover all diseases. The timeliness of such reporting is also a concern.

> **e. Legal Force.** The existing CBMs are politically binding. Current WHO reporting is also politically binding. Outbreak reporting needs to be legally binding.

> **f. Timing.** There ware potential conflicts in timing between considerations by the AHG of outbreaks and the WHO approach to syndrome reporting under revised IHR.

**g. Manpower.** The WHO on a daily basis addresses about a dozen cases of disease outbreaks using teams of experts and with the ability to send, when invited, different teams to different places to investigate outbreaks. A manpower of the order of 100s may be involved at different levels -- WHO headquarters, regional, subregional and national levels. In contrast the BTWC Organization is likely to have a total strength of about 200 to 250 with perhaps a half dozen outbreak specialists. There needs to be cooperation between the BTWC Organization and the WHO.

**h. Cooperation.** This is a difficult subject as there is the potential to cause harm to both the future BTWC Protocol and to the future WHO IHR.

## 5. Ad Hoc Group -- Solutions

In considering solutions to the above challenges, the Ad Hoc Group would need to address some key points which the discussions at the ARW might with advantage also examine. These are:

**a. Legally Binding Requirements.** Is it necessary to go beyond politically binding requirements -- but what was realistically possible?

**b. Reporting and Surveillance.** Much would depend on what information was available on reports of and into outbreaks of disease.

**c. Delineation.** The difficulties of differentiating between natural and unnatural causes of outbreaks was a concern to the NAM. Developing countries are concerned that because of the high number of naturally occurring outbreaks of endemic diseases there may be more of a burden on them.

**d. Cooperation.** It would be better not to try to negotiate the detail as part of the Protocol but rather to have a generic requirement in the Protocol leaving the details to the PrepCom.

**e. Scientific & Technical Cooperation.** Because of the dual use nature of pathogens, the strengthening of reporting and surveillance have very important public health benefits. These are extremely important for developing countries and consequently an important scientific and technical cooperation measure for Article X would be the strengthening of global, regional and national elements of reporting and surveillance.

## 6. Conclusion

The NATO ARW is timely in that it would enable informed debate between scientific and technical specialists and the experts engaged in the delegations to the Ad Hoc Group about these important issues which lie at the heart of an effective future Protocol to strengthen the BTWC. It is important to identify and explore possible solutions.

# THE AGENTS OF CONCERN

PROFESSOR ROQUE MONTELEONE-NETO
*Federal University of Sao Paulo*
*Centre for Medical Informatics*
*Sao Paulo, SP,*
*Brazil*

## 1.  Introduction

The answer to the question of what agents are of concern requires an understanding of the context in which the question is asked.  Specifically, we need to know to whom the agents are of concern and for what reason they are of concern.  Only then can we approach the question of how the concern is to be dealt with in the particular context under discussion.

## 2.  Concern to Whom?

The context for our purposes here is the negotiation to strengthen the Biological and Toxin Weapons Convention (BTWC).  The parties to whom the matter is of concern are therefore the 140 plus States Parties to the BTWC and the Signatory States to the Convention.  Although these states are involved in the common endeavour of the negotiations, it has to be recognised that these states have different sizes and populations, different cultures, different political systems and have different environments and social-economic levels of development.

## 3.  Concern for What?

In the context of the BTWC negotiations the reason why agents may be of concern is in regard to:

-    Declarations (work with listed agents);
-    Import / Export controls;
-    Investigations;
-    Declarations (notifications) of disease outbreaks;
-    Investigations of disease outbreaks / alleged use.

It should be noted that lists of agents can be found for similar purposes in other contexts for example:

-    UNSCOM;
     -    Declarations and export control;
-    Australia Group;
     -    Export controls;

*M. Dando et al. (eds.),*
*Scientific and Technical Means of Distinguishing Between Natural and Other Outbreaks of Disease, 31–34.*
© 2001 *Kluwer Academic Publishers.*

Tables 1, 2, and 3 provide a comparison of the numbers of different types of agents in the list produced by the Ad Hoc Group negotiating the Protocol to the BTWC after the 11th Session (Table 1), the Australia Group list (Table 2), and the UNSCOM list (Table 3).

### Table 1 AD HOC GROUP (up to the 11th session)

|  | Viruses | Bacteria | Fungi | Rickettsiae | Toxins | Total |
|---|---|---|---|---|---|---|
| Human | 17 | 9 | 1 | 3 | 21 | 51 |
| Animal | 18 | | | | | 18 |
| Plants | 20 | | | | | 20 |
| Total | | | | | | 89 |

### Table 2 Australia Group

|  | Viruses | Bacteria | Fungi | Rickettsiae | Toxins | Total |
|---|---|---|---|---|---|---|
| Human Core | 20 | 13 | 0 | 4 | 11 | 48 |
| Warning | 8 | 5 | 0 | 0 | 7 | 20 |
| Animal | 15 | 3 | 0 | 0 | 0 | 18 |
| Plant Core | 0 | 2 | 6 | 0 | 0 | 8 |
| Warning | 1 | 2 | 2 | 0 | 0 | 5 |
| Total Core | 35 | 18 | 6 | 4 | 11 | 74 |
| Warning | 9 | 7 | 2 | 0 | 7 | 25 |

**Table 3 UNSCOM Biological Agents Lists based on the classification in the World Health Organization (WHO) Laboratory Biosafety Manual**

| | Viruses | Bacteria | Myco-plasma | Fungi | Rickettsiae | Toxins | Total |
|---|---|---|---|---|---|---|---|
| LIST 1: Human, Animal and Plant | 36 | 21 | 1 | 6 | 4 | 15 | 83 |
| LIST 2: Human and Animal | 69 | 107 | 0 | 0 | 7 | 0 | 183 |
| Other Animal | 82 | | | | | | 82 |
| Plant Pathogens | 14 | | | | | | 14 |
| Toxins | Other than specified on List 1 with a molecular weight of more than 250 daltons | | | | | | ? |
| Other Organisms | Eukaryotic (non-microbial) organisms which produce any toxin | | | | | | ? |
| TOTAL | | | | | | | > 362 |

It is evident that there are considerable differences between these different lists produced in different contexts.

## 4. Disease outbreaks / alleged use

Turning then to the question of disease outbreaks, a particular issue is the nature of the relationship between the States Parties and the future BTWC organisation set up to implement the Protocol.

In regard to declarations (notification) of disease outbreaks there are a number of issues to be addressed:

- what diseases to declare
  - all
  - natural
  - unnatural;
- when to declare
  - timing in relation to the outbreak;
- economic and social imports
  - tourism, trade consequences;
- the relationship to compliance.

Similarly, in regard to possible investigations of disease outbreaks, issues to be addressed include:

- criteria for establishing a compliance concern;
- policy regarding the possession of samples and access to affected individuals;
- need for assistance and security of the area / region;
- policy regarding involvement of other organisations such as WHO, FAO, OIE, ICRC and others, such as NGOs.

## 5. Conclusions

Whilst these are complex questions it is possible to draw some preliminary conclusions:

- The issue of disease outbreaks of concern to the BWC is related to listed pathogens of concern.
- The relationship between the SP and the BTWO shall address disease outbreaks whether or not they are related to listed pathogens.
- For declarations / notification purposes each SP should declare any outbreaks of disease caused by listed pathogens whether endemic or not in its territory. These declarations should be reviewed every 5 years.
- The SP should immediately notify disease outbreaks caused by listed pathogens to the BTWO. In case of failure to do so, and after [...] days of its [public knowledge], the Executive Council should have the right to approve an investigation.
- Disease outbreaks related to non-listed pathogens should be annually declared. Such outbreaks should only cause a compliance concern if a SP has fundamental suspicions that this event is related to activities prohibited by the Convention, and the request for an investigation is approved by the Executive Council.
- Disease outbreaks related to unknown pathogens shall be treated the same way as the outbreaks related to listed pathogens.
- All information related to disease outbreaks shall have the most stringent degree of confidentiality.

# NATURAL OUTBREAKS OF DISEASE: COMMUNICABLE DISEASE SURVEILLANCE IN THE CZECH REPUBLIC

B. KRIZ, AND J. KYNCL
*Centre of Epidemiology and Microbiology,*
*National Institute of Public Health,*
*Prague,*
*Czech Republic*

## 1. Introduction

Infectious diseases represent great danger for human health. Surveillance of diseases is a method that can partly solve this threat and contribute to health improvement. Fundamental elements of surveillance are data collection, analysis, interpretation and distribution of information. Communicable disease surveillance in the Czech Republic has a long history.

## 2. Early History

First mentions of anti-epidemic measures and statistical investigation organised in the Czech lands date back to the time of the Emperor Rudolph II (1576 – 1611). In 1583, an extensive plague epidemic resulted in about 20,000 victims in Prague. The Czech Diet reacted to that situation by asking the imperial chamber to designate four physicians (more precisely to allocate funds for their salaries) "who, as the kingdom physicians, would surveil the beginnings of general diseases, would prevent them from spreading and would report on them". Institution of this service was further extended by designation of four auxiliary physicians, "magistri sanitatis", in the cities in time of epidemics whose role was, among others, "to make the population aware of the police rules in case of an epidemic outbreak". The Czech Kingdom was the first country to implement such measures. Only later, such institutions were established in the other countries of the Austro-Hungarian monarchy.

In the 19th century, the notification of infectious diseases was progressively extended to any physician. The court decree of November 3, 1808 established that "the general practitioner has to notify the paramount authority of an epidemic outbreak among the population or of plague cases in cattle" and it was underlined that he should not wait till the epidemic or plague spread but has to notify the first 4, 6 or 8 cases in humans or animals recorded in a locality (according to its size). Later, many different regulations instructed both the physicians and population to notify occurrence of infectious diseases. Also the procedure to be followed in investigation of epidemics and the measures to be taken were established.

35

*M. Dando et al. (eds.),*
*Scientific and Technical Means of Distinguishing Between Natural and Other Outbreaks of Disease, 35–39.*
© 2001 *Kluwer Academic Publishers.*

The proof that this system was really operational in the 1880's is the "Report on public health conditions and activities of the city health office of Prague of 1882" showing that the following diseases were notified: scarlet fever, diphtheria, measles, pertussis, exanthematous typhus and smallpox. An extensive part of this report is the "List of houses affected by infectious diseases" where addresses and number of cases of and deaths from different infections are given for the whole of Prague.

## 3. The Later 19th Century

The year 1888 can be considered as the actual start of an operational system of notification of infectious diseases: the Ministry of Interior Affairs issued a regulation which established the notification of infectious diseases.

The first publication to summarise notification data on the diseases mentioned above was the "Report on public health conditions in the Czech kingdom in 1892" issued by Dr. Hynek Pelc, the regional public health officer and president of the regional public health council. The incidence of different infections was calculated according to political districts. The following data were given: number of the communities affected, number of population of each community, absolute number of cases, relative number of cases per 1000 population, percentage of the adults affected, absolute mortality, lethality, percentage of the adults dead and duration of the epidemic. A table summarised the seasonal incidence data. In addition to the tabular data, the spread of infection was described. The most serious infection in children was diphtheria with a lethality rate of 40.2 %.

## 4. The 20th Century

The whole issue of anti-epidemic measures, including notification of other infectious diseases, was addressed comprehensively in a particular imperial act of April 14, 1913 known as the Epidemic Law. It consisted of five parts: "disease diagnosis, measures to prevent notifiable diseases, compensation of expenses resulting from the measures taken, penal regulations, and general regulations". The following 17 infections were notifiable: smallpox, cholera, plague, exanthematous typhus, scarlet fever, diphtheria, epidemic meningitis, diarrhoea, typhoid fever, anthrax, glanders, rabies including injury caused by an animal with suspected rabies, leprosy, yellow fever, recrudescent typhus, trachoma, and puerperal fever. In addition, measles, pertussis, parotitis, rubella, and chickenpox were notifiable in nursing and boarding homes. In 1917 – 1920, malaria, chickenpox, influenza, poliomyelitis, lethargic encephalitis and paratyphoid fever were added to the list of notifiable diseases. These infectious diseases continued to be notified the same way up to 1945.

Notification of each case of the infections mentioned above was requested from the physicians who had diagnosed it, but also from the midwives, householders or administrators of institutes or schools of all sorts, hostel owners, house owners, and vets. Notifiable data included patient's given name, surname, age, address and disease. These data were notified to the mayor who had to submit them without delay to the district authority. The first five cases of serious diseases were to be notified telegraphically or by phone free of charge, the following cases were notified on particular forms by mail free of charge.

At the very beginning of the century, bacteriological and serological investigations were carried out by the national investigative institutes. The principles of infectious material sampling and mailing were established. "Each consignment is required to be placed in three containers (of glass, metal and wood) and then wrapped in paper and labelled with the address and a cross."

Relatively extensive was the part of the law dealing with the measures to be taken in case of infectious diseases, i.e., patient's isolation, transfer to hospital, disaffection, disinsection, possible disposal of patient's personal things and animal carcasses, ways of compensation and expenses reimbursement.

The 1920's and 1930's saw the rapid development of microbiology both in the field of diagnosis and vaccine research and development. New knowledge in epidemiology of infectious diseases and new possibilities in their prevention and Prophylaxis led to their decreased incidence or even elimination (smallpox). Nevertheless, the World War II meant discontinuation of this progress and re-emergence of some serious infections.

## 5. The Reporting System Today

Contemporary reporting system for infectious disease surveillance in the Czech Republic has these levels:

1. district level – District Public Health Service,
2. regional level – Regional Public Health Service,
3. national level – National Institute of Public Health, Ministry of Health.

There is regular weekly reporting using computerised system EPIDAT and monthly written reporting with data form and comments. Irregular reporting by phone or fax is used immediately in case of an important single case or outbreaks. Epidemiological investigation of selected single infections and all outbreaks including microbiological results and setting up measures starts at District Public Health Service. National Reference Laboratories provide specialised microbiological investigations.

Program EPIDAT was created to ensure notification, registration and analysis of morbidity due to infections. Since 1993, the EPIDAT has been used nation-wide by all public health services. The EPIDAT is part of the National Health Information System and is the basis of local, regional and national surveillance of infectious diseases. It is a health information system based on notification by attending physicians and those of public health service. The program has been written using the programs of the EPI-INFO system of the WHO and CDC in Atlanta. The system consists of several interdependent sections allowing data entry at a district level, data coding, data transmission and merging at a regional level and at the National Institute of Public Health, and major analyses for different periods. Data are entered continuously, data export is performed at one-week intervals, transmissions are executed by e-mail and outputs are weekly. The input and output files are referred to the National Institute of Public Health where the access rights are treated. The data transmitted are encoded.

Data are entered according to the lists of admissible variables displayed one by one on the screen. General data include name, address, age, sex, date of first signs, diagnosis, reporting profession and place. Special data are according to diagnosis: vaccination, clinical symptoms, source of infection, transmission, results of microbiological investigation and others. Any record can be cancelled any time (e.g., if the initial diagnosis is not confirmed) and conversely, any record cancelled can be renewed any time. The record can also be adapted according to the facts newly revealed. All forms in which any change was made are automatically referred to a higher level. Any sentence changed, cancelled or renewed at the District Public Health Service will be modified accordingly in the databases of the Regional Public Health Service and that of the National Institute of Public Health.

According to the epidemiological criteria, the diagnoses notified by the EPIDAT are divided into eight groups with similar questionnaires:

- Alimentary infections $1^{st}$ type (typhoid fever, salmonellosis, shigellosis);
- Alimentary infections $2^{nd}$ type (infectious enteritis and alimentary intoxications);
- Vaccination schedule infections (i.e., infections against which the population of the Czech Republic is regularly vaccinated and some others against which vaccination is foreseen in the future);
- Viral hepatitis;
- CNS infections (meningococci, tick-borne encephalitis);
- Zoonoses not included in the previous groups (rabies, leptospirosis, tularemia, listeriosis, campylobacteriosis);
- Parasitic and mycotic infections;
- Others infections monitored.

In the Czech Republic there also exists reporting system for another diseases such as:

- acute respiratory infections including influenza;
- HIV / AIDS;
- tuberculosis;
- sexually transmitted diseases.

## 6. Conclusion

General principles for infectious disease surveillance can be from the point of view of the legislation be characterised in the following way:

- regular compulsory reporting (disease and outbreaks, epidemics) by general practitioners and medical doctors from outpatient and hospital wards;
- epidemiological investigation of selected diseases and outbreaks by epidemiologists;
- vaccine coverage (significant sample) by control, done by epidemiologists;
- isolation of selected diseases on infections wards;
- noncompulsory reporting of diseases by microbiologists;
- noncompulsory elements: serological surveys and other studies.

For selected diseases special national surveillance programmes were formulated and published, including all necessary elements like:

- definition, probable case, clinically proved, epidemiologicaly proved, laboratory proved;
- imported or indigenous case;
- laboratory tests – examination and confirmation;
- measures in case of a single case;
- measures in case of an outbreak.

Czech national system of outbreak management consists of:

- report by phone, made by the physician who first diagnosed the suspicion of the outbreak;
- District Public Health Service (Dept. of Epidemiology) organises epidemiological investigation in cooperation with clinicians and laboratories;
- at the same time District Public Health Service (Dept. of Epidemiology) organises the epidemic measures;
- report by phone, fax or e-mail to Regional Public Health Service, National Institute of Public Health, Ministry of Health;
- National Institute of Public Health gives support in resolution of epidemiologicaly significant situation.

The National system of communicable disease surveillance is based on functional local surveillance. This system is managed in accordance with specific conditions and is orientated to effective measures.

# DISTINGUISHING BETWEEN NATURAL DISEASE OUTBREAKS AND DELIBERATE ATTACKS ON HUMAN BEINGS USING BIOLOGICAL WEAPONS

MALCOLM DANDO AND SIMON WHITBY
*Department of Peace Studies,*
*University of Bradford,*
*Bradford, BD7 1DP*
*West Yorkshire, UK*

## 1. Introduction

In order to consider how it might be possible to distinguish between a natural outbreak of disease in a human population and a deliberate attack using biological weapons it is necessary to begin by outlining the characteristics of a deliberate attack. Here we attempt to outline such characteristics by reviewing a number of possible attack scenarios the might be made by non-state, sub-state and state actors. From these scenarios we then draw out a series of characteristics which would occur. These characteristics are then compared and contrasted with the characteristics of natural outbreaks and conclusions are drawn as to the possibility of distinguishing between these two different cases.

## 2. Scenarios

In his discussion of different types of biological attacks against humans Wheelis[1] considered three scales of release of agent: a point source, medium scale and large scale. He argued that an individual might be able to cause a point source or medium scale release in criminal acts, but would not be able to cause a large scale release of biological agent. Similarly a sub-national group could carry out a point source release or a medium- scale release in an assassination attempt or a terrorist act. Such a group, however, might also be capable of military use of biological agents involving large-scale releases in, for example, a war of national liberation. Clearly, a State could carry out all three levels of biological agent release and all these different kinds of operations.

We can summarise these possibilities in Table 2.1.

**Table 2.1 Possibilities of different kinds of actors carrying out different levels of biological weapons attacks.**

|  | Non-State | Sub-State | State |
|---|---|---|---|
| Point source | Yes | Yes | Yes |
| Medium scale | Possible | Possible | Yes |
| Large scale | Unlikely | Unlikely | Yes |

41

*M. Dando et al. (eds.),*
*Scientific and Technical Means of Distinguishing Between Natural and Other Outbreaks of Disease,* 41–47.
© 2001 *Kluwer Academic Publishers.*

What is of interest here, in particular, is that Wheelis also noted that some of these many different kinds of operations might involve the perpetrators wishing to act covertly. It is possible to imagine that people carrying out a criminal/terrorist act, such as that attempted by the Bhagwan Shree Rajneesh sect in Oregon in 1984,[2] would not wish to be traced. Indeed, it is possible that a State which had carried out an act of aggression might wish to prevent interference from the international community by mounting a large-scale attack against forces and facilities building up in its region without its involvement being clear.

The available evidence would suggest strongly that provided adequate public health records were kept and investigators had reasonable access in good time it would be difficult for a criminal[3] or terrorist[4] act to be carried out covertly against an individual or group of people without a grave risk of exposure. Modern civil societies do have a great deal of experience in dealing with natural public health risks and natural disease outbreaks that would form a distinctive normal background against which attempted covert acts could be judged as being caused by human actions.

What is of interest here, however, is whether there is any reason to believe that a large-scale release of a biological agent – say by a regional aggressor in the scenario previously described – could be carried out without grave risk of detection.

### 3. Military Usage of Biological Agents

Should the military requirement be for a rapid action then the probable biological agent of choice would be a bacterial toxin, but if a longer delay was acceptable then a living bacterial or viral agent might be deployed.

### 3.1 BOTULINUM TOXIN

In a detailed analysis of "Defense Against Toxin Weapons" the US Army *Textbook of Military Medicine* concluded that[5]:

> "Because there are hundreds of toxins available in nature, the job of protecting troops against them seems overwhelming. It might seem that an aggressor would need only to discover the toxins against which we can protect our troops, and then pick a different one to weaponise..."

The account continues to point out, however, that it would not be that simple for an attacker:

> "...The ability of toxins as MCBWs [Mass Casualty Biological (Toxin) Weapons] is limited by their toxicity. The criterion alone reduces the list of potential open-air weaponsizable toxins for MCBWs from hundreds to fewer than 20..."

The accompanying table shows, in fact, that there are 17 most toxic toxins – all originating from bacteria. The most toxin toxins are defined as having an $LD_{50}$ (lethal dose for 50 per cent of an exposed population) of $0.025\mu g/kg$ (micrograms/kilograms).

**Table 3.1  Categorisation of Toxins by Toxicity**

| Source of Toxin | Number of Toxins in Each Category | | | |
|---|---|---|---|---|
| | Most Toxic (LD50 <0.025µg/kg) | Highly Toxic (0.025-2.5µg/kg) | Moderately Toxic (2.5 µg/kg) | Total |
| Bacteria | 17 | 12 | >20 | >49 |
| Plant | – | 5 | >31 | >36 |
| Fungi | – | – | >26 | >26 |
| Marine Organisms | | >46 | >65 | >111 |
| Snakes | – | 8 | >116 | >124 |
| Algae | – | 2 | >20 | >22 |
| Insects | – | – | >22 | >22 |
| Amphibians | – | – | >5 | > 5 |
| Total | 17 | >73 | >305 | >395 |

As the account notes "An armoured or infantry division in the field is not a great risk of exposure to a marine toxin whose toxicity is so low that 80 tonnes is needed to produce a MCBW covering $10km^2$."

A paper produced by the United States in 1992 for the VEREX meeting considering possible verification measures for the Biological and Toxin Weapons Convention gives an idea of the amounts of much more toxic toxins that would be required[6]. The research on which the paper was based assumed that the toxin would be dispersed in the air below a 100 – meter ceiling and that people would be breathing at a rate of 12 litres per minute. It also assumed that a military base would occupy an area of 10 $km^2$, a city 1,000 $km^2$ and a battlefield 3,000 $km^2$. A table then indicated the amounts of toxin that would be needed for various attack scenarios under certain assumptions about the toxicity of the toxin and the efficiency of dispersal of the agent. Using conservative estimates of 100mg as the $LD_{50}$ level for individuals and a dispersal efficiency of 1% for the agent, it was suggested that the amount of material required to attack a base would be 10 gms and to attack a city or battlefield 10kg or 30kg respectively.

These might seem very small amounts of material, but if the attack was successful, and the victims had not been immunised against the toxin beforehand a very large number of people would quickly begin to exhibit symptoms which medical staff would not have too much difficulty in suspecting as possibly (inhalation) botulism,[7] and in such circumstances collecting samples for testing with sensitive enzyme – linked immunosorbent assays would surely be undertaken. Moreover, given the area over which victims were being located a natural event would hardly seem probable. In such circumstances a thoroughgoing investigation of the circumstances would surely be initiated by the affected parties. The likely outcome of such an investigation if large numbers of people were shown to have come down with symptoms of inhalation botulism over a wide area, and all closely associated in time, could be expected to be a conclusion pointing to a biological attack.

## 3.2 ANTHRAX

A calculation of the amount of anthrax that would be required for a militarily significant clandestine stand-off attack at night was given by Bartlett in 1996.[8] He argued that the attacker would need to release of the order of $10^{12}ID_{50}$ (where $ID_{50}$ was the dose required to infect 50 percent of an exposed population). He suggested, moreover, that this "trillion dose criterion" would also apply for other scenarios and could therefore be regarded as widely applicable for normal military purposes.

The calculation used the base model for a long line source where the dose received, (D), was assumed to be:

$$D = {}^{Q.b}\!/_{h\bar{u}}$$

Q in this equation being the source strength (units/m), b the breathing rate (volume/min), h the depth of the air mixing layer and $\bar{u}$ the mean surface wind speed.

Typical values are as follows according to this paper:

$b = 20$ litres/min $= 2 \times 10^{-2}$ m$^3$ min$^{-1}$

$h = 1$ km $\qquad = 10^3$m

$\bar{u} = 3$ m/s $\qquad = 3 \times 10^2$ m min$^{-1}$

Therefore it is argued for D = 10 $ID_{50}$

$$Q = \frac{10.10^3.\ 3 \times 10^2}{2 \times 10^{-2}} \quad = \quad 1.5 \times 10^8\ ID_{50}$$

Thus the attacker needs to achieve, according to this calculation, about $10^8$ $ID_{50}$/m. So for a 10 km line source this is equivalent to $10^4 \times 10^8$ $ID_{50}$ which equals the trillion dose criterion of $10^{12}$ $ID_{50}$.

A proliferator using a bacterial fermenter could be fairly confident of achieving a concentration of about $10^8$ bacterial cells / ml. So to reach the trillion dose criterion he would need to grow:

$10^{12}$ x (Number of cells equivalent to ID 50)
($10^8$ x 1000) litres of suspension.

In the case of *B. anthracis*, the causative agent of anthrax, the $ID_{50}$ for man is estimated to be about $10^4$ cells. Thus the total quantity of culture required, if these assumptions hold, would be 100,000 litres.

This, of course, is a not insignificant amount of material, and the author points out that most infectious agents would likely be less robust in the environment so the proliferator would have to compensate by balancing the amount required to ensure a similar effect on distribution of the agent.

Anthrax agent used effectively in this way would again produce recognisable symptoms[9] in unvaccinated people across a very wide area in a common time period. Thus it could be expected that the event would be investigated as intensively as in the botulinum toxin case above and that the conclusion of the investigation would be that an attack had taken place.

## 3.3 MILITARY-RELATED ATTACKS

A regional aggressor in the scenario described above might, or course, decide that there was far too much risk of retaliation if a massive attack with biological weapons was made against the deployed forced of the international community. Whilst the perpetrator of such an attack might not be certain, the possible candidate would be obvious. In such circumstances a lesser attack directed at the civilian population of a major city might be considered. If the city contained the major supply centres for the deployed force sufficient disruption might be caused to have militarily-significant consequences, but, probably more important, there could be political consequences in regard to the stability of the international coalition and the desire of its local ally to evade further attacks/disease outbreaks.

A potential scenario is described in the SIPRI Yearbook of 2000.[10] In the study described an amount of aerosolised respirable anthrax spores thought to be the equivalent to the release at Sverdlovosk was effectively released over a 15–minutes period from a road 15 metres above street level. It was assumed that a wind of about 4.5 metres per second was blowing the spores at a height of 10 metres above the target shopping mall. It was further assumed that as the efficiency of the distribution system was only 5 per cent. Thus, 80 billion respirable spores would have to have been released to generate the 4 billion effective spores. Whilst some 20,000-30,000 people could have been exposed with standard respiration rates and $ID_{50}$ for anthrax, the FOA model used with the concentration of people in the street, assumed to be 0.2 person/m$^2$, suggested that some 300 people would be infected.

Clearly, if the attack was carried out covertly and no treatment was given until the symptoms became clear days later, panic amongst the civilian population would be a likely outcome. The situation would be far worse, or course, if an agent infective from the first victim, such as plague, was used. What is interesting about the SIPRI study from the point of view of concealment of the attack is the comment that:

> "...a relatively large fraction of the spores would be deposited on the street, roofs, walls and other surfaces...the authorities would face a huge decontamination problem."

In short, an investigation of this level of attack would likely to be rapidly initiated and also be likely to come to the robust conclusion that the outbreak was not natural.

## 4. Characteristics of Biological Attacks

The scenarios described suggest that medium and large-scale attacks would have certain clear characteristics. The dispersal of the agent over a large geographical area simultaneously would lead to multiple parallel casualties spread over a particular location. If the agent was not infective from the first victim the disease would be seen to be spread over time from the release. If an infective agent (from the first victim) was used it would be clear that there were multiple sources of the continuing outbreak not a single or small number of sources as in a natural outbreak.

A detailed investigation of the outbreak would naturally look closely at the strain of the agent involved. A weaponised agent would probably have been carefully selected for its particular characteristics suitable for weaponisation and likely would not therefore be endemic to the region. The increasing capabilities for subspecies identification would clearly make the task of carrying out a covert attack more and more difficult.

## 5. Conclusion

Now it might be argued that an attacker could further scale down the weight of his assault in order that the outbreak was much closer to, and therefore much more difficult to distinguish from, a natural outbreak. Whilst this is surely correct, it does expose an inescapable contradiction for the attacker: the more the attack was scaled down to render it convert and indistinguishable from a natural outbreak the more likely the public health system would be able to cope with the problem – and the less likely any desired political/military outcome.

Thus it seems likely that there is always going to be a problem for an attacker using biological weapons on any appreciable scale against human beings – it is likely to be seen as a biological weapons attack if any reasonable social order is in place and any reasonably effective investigation can be carried out. An exception to such a conclusion might, for example, be an attack carried out in the chaos of all-out warfare between sub-state factions after the degeneration of effective central systems of public health and political control.

Such an exception also points the way to better ensuring that biological warfare against humans is further deterred. The better the public health systems in place around the world and the better and more complete the reporting of natural disease outbreaks the less likely it is that an attack with biological weapons would be carried out covertly.

## Notes

[1]  Wheelis, M. (1997) *Addressing the Full Range of Biological Warfare in a BWC Compliance Protocol.* Paper presented to Pugwash Meeting No. 229, 20-21 September.

[2]  Török, T. *et al* (1999) A large community outbreak of salmonellosis caused by intentional contamination of restaurant salad bars. *Biological Warfare: Limiting the Threat*, Lederberg, J (Ed.), pp 167-184, The MIT Press, Cambridge.

[3]  Knight, B. (1979) Ricin – A potent homicidal poison. *British Medical Journal*, 3, (February), 35-51.

[4]  Carus, W.S. (1999) Unlawful acquisition and use of biological agents, pp 211-232, in Lederberg, J, (as ref 2).

[5]  Franz, D. (1997) Defense against toxin weapons, pp. 603-619 in Sidell, F. R. et al (eds) *Medical Aspects of Chemical and Biological Warfare.* Office of the Surgeon General, Department of the Army, Washington D. C.

[6]  United States, (1992) *Biologically Derived Toxins: Quantities for Legitimate Use.* Ad Hoc Group of Governmental Experts to Identify and Examine Potential Verification Measures from a Scientific and Technical Standpoint. BWC/CONF. III/ VEREX/ WP. 88, Geneva, 4 December.

[7]  Middlebrook, J. L. and Franz, D. (1997) Botulinum Toxins, pp 643-654 in Sidell, F.R., (as Note 5).

[8]  Bartlett, J. T. (1996) *The Arms Control Challenge: Science and Technology Dimension.* Paper presented to a NATO Advanced Research Workshop on "The Technology of Biological Arms Control and Disarmament". Budapest, 28-30 March.

[9]  Friedlander, A. M. (1997) Anthrax. pp 467-478 in Sidell, F. R. , (as Note 5).

[10]  Zanders, J.P. et al (2000) Appendix 9A. Risk assessment of terrorism with chemical and biological weapons. pp 537 – 559 in the *SIPRI Yearbook.* Oxford University Press, Oxford.

world and the better and more complete the reporting of natural disease outbreaks the less likely it is that an attack with biological weapons would be carried out covertly.

# CHARACTERISTICS OF NATURAL OUTBREAKS OF CROP DISEASES

PAUL ROGERS
*Department of Peace Studies*
*University of Bradford*
*Bradford*
*West Yorkshire BD7 1DP, UK*

## 1. The international significance of crops diseases

Losses of crops arising from the effects of other living organisms are grouped into losses due to diseases, pests and weeds. Diseases and pests cause pre- and post-harvest losses, whereas weeds just cause pre-harvest losses. Losses due to all causes can amount to 40% or more of a crop, with pre-harvest losses due to disease usually being around 10-15% of a crop.

This paper is concerned with pre-harvest losses due to plant diseases, whether caused by fungi, bacteria, viruses or mycoplasma, but it concentrates on those diseases which are most likely to lend themselves to be used in anti-crop biological warfare programmes. For the most part, these are air-borne fungal diseases that infect the aerial parts of plants. This specific concern may first be placed in the context of wider aspects of crop losses due to disease.

Table 1 summarises information on losses due to diseases in major groups of crops. Production figures correctly indicate the global importance of the cereal grains, principally rice, wheat, corn (maize) and barley, but underestimate the significance of highly nutritious legume crops and high value beverage crops (coffee, tea and cocoa).

Potatoes and sugarcane are two of the most disease-prone crops. Potatoes experience a wide range of leaf and soil-borne diseases and sugar cane, with its long growth period (up to 20 months) and intensive cropping, is particularly prone to the build-up of many leaf diseases.

## Table 1 World Crop Losses (Pre-Harvest) due to Diseases

| Crop | Production (tons/year) | Crop Loss (percentage) |
|------|------------------------|------------------------|
| Cereals | 1,695 | 9.2 |
| Potatoes | 225 | 21.8 |
| Other root crops | 556 | 16.7 |

*M. Dando et al. (eds.),*
*Scientific and Technical Means of Distinguishing Between Natural and Other Outbreaks of Disease, 49–61.*
© 2001 *Kluwer Academic Publishers.*

| | | |
|---|---|---|
| Sugarcane | 811 | 19.2 |
| Legumes | 45 | 11.3 |
| Other vegetables | 368 | 10.1 |
| Fruits | 302 | 12.6 |
| Beverage crops | 8 | 17.7 |
| Oil crops | 240 | 9.8 |

Most of the world's major crops suffer from severe diseases, and Table 2 gives examples of some of the most significant of these. Bearing in mind the dominant importance of cereals as sources of food, the rusts, smuts and leaf spots of cereals such as rice and wheat must rank as the most important of all diseases of crops.

Crop diseases have been responsible for major economic problems in many countries and, on occasions, have resulted in severe famine killing millions of people. The most notable examples are the Irish potato famine in the 1840s and the Bengal famine in the 1940s, but there are many other examples.

Coffee leaf rust resulted in the destruction of most coffee growing in Asia in the late nineteenth century. It also explains the English propensity for drinking tea, since colonial possessions such as Ceylon and India concentrated on growing tea in place of coffee. When coffee leaf rust spread to Latin America in the early 1970s, it spread rapidly through plantations throughout the sub-continent as bushes were susceptible to the disease, unlike coffee varieties in Africa which were largely resistant.

**Table 2. Selected Examples of Severe Plant Disease Losses**

| Disease | Location | Notes |
|---|---|---|
| *Fungal Diseases* | | |
| Cereal rusts | World-wide | Frequent severe epidemics with huge annual losses. |
| Cereal smuts | World-wide | Continuous losses affecting all cereals. |
| Late blight of potato | Cool, temperate | Epidemics - main cause of Irish famine, recent problems in North America. |
| Brown spot of rice | Asia | Epidemics including the Bengal famine of 1943. |
| Southern corn leaf blight | United States | $1 b loss in 1970 epidemic. |
| Coffee leaf rust | Now world-wide | Destroyed coffee in Southeast Asia in 1870s/80s, epidemics in Latin America since 1970. |
| Banana Sigatoka leaf spot | World-wide | Heavy losses each year. |
| Dutch Elm disease | Europe and North America | Most European elms killed; |

| | | |
|---|---|---|
| | | destroying most North American elms since 1930. |
| *Virus diseases* | | |
| Sugarcane mosaic | World-wide | Heavy losses on sugarcane and corn. |
| Swollen shoot of cacao (cocoa) | Africa | Continuous heavy losses. |
| Barley yellow dwarf | World-wide | Causes problems in small grains in many countries. |
| *Bacterial diseases* | | |
| Citrus canker | Asia, Africa, the Americas | Millions of trees killed in Florida in 1910s and major problem in the 1980s. |
| Fire blight of apples, pears, etc. | Europe and North America | Heavy annual losses - kills trees. |

Not all crop diseases spread rapidly - those on perennial crops can be slow-moving but with a ultimately disastrous effects. Dutch elm disease has progressively killed most elm trees in Britain and the United States, but has taken several decades to do so.

It is possible to obtain an assessment of the relative importance of crop diseases, pests and weeds in different regions of the world, and this is summarised in Table 3. As might be expected, control is more effective, and losses lower, in countries with well-developed agricultural extension services and crop protection capabilities. Thus Europe and North America experience losses substantially lower than those of Africa and Asia.

**Table 3. Crop Losses by Region - % loss to diseases, pests and weeds**

| | |
|---|---|
| Europe | 25 |
| Australasia | 28 |
| North and Central America | 29 |
| Former Soviet Union and China | 30 |
| South America | 33 |
| Africa | 42 |
| Asia | 43 |
| South America | 33 |
| Africa | 42 |
| Asia | 43 |

Plant pathology has developed as a branch of the life sciences over at least a century, and it might therefore be thought that most crop diseases are readily amenable to control, that losses due to crop diseases are diminishing and that major new problems are unlikely to occur. The evidence suggests otherwise, and Table 4 illustrates some of the recent and current problems of crop disease, mainly a consequence of diseases spreading to new regions. These are in addition to new virulent strains of diseases affecting existing areas of production, as with the problems arising from new strains of late blight of potatoes in North America (Table 2).

**Table 4. Recent and Current Disease Problems**

| | |
|---|---|
| Downy mildew of corn | Spreading from South-East Asia (maize) and sorghum. |
| Soybean rust | Spreading mainly from South-East Asia. |
| African cassava mosaic | A potential threat in Asia and the Americas. |
| Bacterial wilt of bananas | Destructive in the Americas, spreading elsewhere. |
| Bunchy top of bananas | Destructive in Asia-Pacific and parts of Africa, potentially destructive in the Americas. |
| Lethal yellowing of coconut palm | Destructive in Central America and spreading out. |

**2. The Particular Significance of Fungal Diseases for Biological Warfare**

Diseases caused by mycoplasma and viruses can spread rapidly, especially when there is an airborne arthropod vector, but most such diseases build up fairly slowly. Bacterial diseases are commonly soil-borne, and while some of the non-soil-borne bacterial diseases can spread rapidly, most soil-borne bacterial diseases are only capable of a slow rate of spread. Soil-borne diseases can devastate crops, but because they increase in intensity over a number of growing seasons, they are not normally considered to be appropriate agents of anti-crop warfare.

There are also many soil-borne fungal diseases which are similarly rather slow to spread, and evidence from knowledge of past anti-BW programmes[1] indicates that the emphasis has been an air-borne diseases. Furthermore, the evidence, though limited, suggests that the main area of concentration has been on those fungal diseases of major food crops that are prone to rapidly developing epidemics within a single growing season. This paper therefore aims simply to discuss the features of naturally occurring plant disease epidemics with an emphasis on those particular kinds of diseases.

# 3. Components of a Plant Disease Epidemic

The five components of an epidemic in cultivated crops are:

- the host plant
- the pathogen
- the environment
- human activity
- time

## 3.1 THE HOST PLANT

For an epidemic to develop, the host plant must be present in a concentration sufficient for the pathogen to move easily from plant to plant, and it must be susceptible to the particular race of the pathogen present. Furthermore, there should be a genetic uniformity within the crop. A genetically heterogeneous crop will have individuals with highly variable resistance, hindering the development of the epidemic - natural populations of plants rarely experience epidemic disease losses.

Within developed country agriculture, there is a tendency to rely on very few varieties of any particular crop. While such varieties may be resistant to the diseases endemic to the country concerned, this can entail considerable susceptibility to newly introduced diseases. Table 5 summarises data for major US crops.

**Table 5  Crop Acre Dominance by Varieties (United States)**

| Crop | Acreage (m) | Major varieties | Acreage (%) |
|------|-------------|-----------------|-------------|
| Cotton | 11.2 | 3 | 53 |
| Corn (maize) | 66.3 | 6 | 71 |
| Peas | 0.4 | 2 | 96 |
| Potatoes | 1.4 | 4 | 72 |
| Soybean | 42.4 | 6 | 56 |
| Sugar beet | 1.4 | 2 | 42 |
| Wheat | 44.3 | 9 | 50 |

54

The development of a plant disease epidemic is heavily influenced by the relative susceptibility of the host crop at different stages of its life. Some diseases affect crops only when they have just germinated, others when they are young and still others only when the crop is mature. A few diseases affect a crop both early and late in its growth. For most diseases on most crops, the period of early maturity of a crop, when it is completing or has just completed its most intensive growth phase is also the period when it is most resistant to diseases. In Figure 1, Graph I shows a plant susceptible at germination (a) and in early growth (b), Graph II shows a plant susceptible in maturity and Graph III shows a plant susceptible at more than one stage.

**Figure 1 Susceptibility Charts**[2]

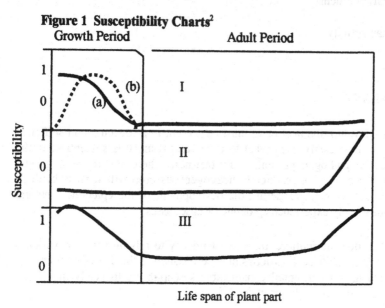

Life span of plant part

## 3.2 THE PATHOGEN

The intensity of the epidemic will depend on the virulence of the pathogen - its speed of infection, spread and reproduction, and the extent to which these ensure a fast rate of production of inoculum for further infection. The core point is that the more sources of infection that are available when plants are susceptible, the more serious the epidemic.

The original source of an infection, early in the growing season, may take several forms. A common reservoir of infection is spores surviving in the soil from the previous season. Another reservoir can be diseased material that is not destroyed at the end of a growing season - blighted potato tubers left in piles by the side of a field can form an important reservoir for the following year's infection. Some plant pathogens have complex life histories that involve alternate hosts. In such circumstances, it is even possible for a wild population of plants of a different species to the crop to provide a reservoir for infection. It is also possible that a pathogen can over-winter on a crop in one region and spread to another region on different varieties of the crop planted in the spring.

The mode of spread of a pathogen is frequently crucial to the development of an epidemic. Pathogens that infect plants through the leaves, spread rapidly in the plant and produce spores which are then blown by the wind to other plants, are likely to demonstrate rapid disease spread, but flying insect vectors can also result in rapid spread. A common form of spread is **splash dispersal** where rain falls on infected leaves and splashes spores on to nearby healthy leaves.

3.3 THE ENVIRONMENT

The development of an epidemic is very often heavily dependent on a wide range of environmental factors, most notably the weather. Many fungal diseases of crops are highly susceptible to quite small changes in temperature, light and humidity, especially in relation to their production of spores. Figure 2 shows spore production in the fungus causing a form of mildew on cereals at 100% relative humidity and a 16 hour day. Diseases spread by splash dispersal are necessarily highly dependent on periods of rain, preferably short sharp showers occurring regularly over a number of days. Weather also influences survival of a pathogen outside of the host - a warm damp winter may allow far more spores to survive in the soil than a hard cold frosty winter.

**Figure 2  Relation of Temperature to Spore Germination**[3]

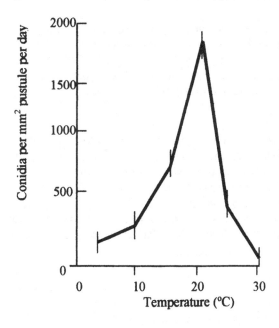

The development of epidemics of late blight of potatoes is very closely related to weather conditions. If a prolonged period of several days of damp cool weather (near 100% RH and 16-22 degrees C) occurs when the potato crop is most vulnerable, an unprotected crop can be destroyed within a couple of weeks. Knowledge of such conditions can make it possible to develop computer-based disease forecasts, allowing control measures to be employed.

Environmental factors also have a significant effect on host susceptibility. Thus a period of drought or cold weather may limit the growth of a pathogen but can also place the host plant under considerable stress, increasing its susceptibility to the disease.

## 3.4 HUMAN ACTIVITY

Of the many effects of human activity which favour the development of epidemics, three are the most significant:

- continuous monoculture of large acreages of crops of a single, potentially susceptible variety,

- the selection of propagative material which is itself diseased,

- failure to control external sources of infection.

The reverse of this, use of disease-free resistant varieties and practice of crop hygiene, including crop rotation, along with biological and chemical disease control, where appropriate, leads to a low likelihood of epidemics. Such practices clearly have economic costs affecting the profitability of a crop, and crop disease control is, to a large extent, a function of balancing costs with advantages based on a sound knowledge of pathogen behaviour.

Broadly speaking, diseases problems are lowest in two forms of arable agriculture. One is "rich country" agriculture where extension services are well developed and intensive crop production is accompanied by detailed if costly attention to disease control. The other form of agriculture, perhaps surprisingly, is "poor country" smallholder agriculture or subsistence farming, where intensive labour makes it feasible to inter-crop many different types of crop in single plots of land, the inter-cropping making it difficult for diseases to spread rapidly from one plant to another across plants of other species.

## 3.5 TIME

The structure of epidemics has been admirably summarised by Agrios:

"Epidemics develop as a consequence of the interactions of the population of their two components, hosts and pathogens, as influenced by environmental and human interference over time. The interactions of hosts and pathogens produce the third component, disease.

Each of these primary components of epidemics consists of subcomponents. The host may be an annual, a perennial, or a tree; it goes through certain growth states (seedling, tillering, blossoming); it is propagated by seed, or vegetatively; it may be resistant or susceptible; it may react by producing lesions or a blight.

The subcomponents of the pathogen include pathogenicity (biotroph, necrotroph, toxins, mode of penetration); virulence (varietal specialisation or race); sporulation (kind and amount of inoculum); dispersal (growth, by wind, water, vectors); and survival (duration, form).

The subcomponents of disease include infection (number of lesions, systemic); pathogenesis (presence and length of incubation period); lesion formation (size, rate, toxins); infectiousness (time and amount of sporulation, amount of new inoculum); spread (infection gradient in host population); multiplication (length of infection cycle, duration and/or number of generations per season); and survival (longevity in months or years).

As we increase our knowledge of the subcomponents of each epidemic, we also increase our ability to predict the pattern of individual epidemics and to interfere at the most appropriate stage of the epidemic with more efficient and more dependable methods of control."

Dependent on the interaction of pathogen and host, disease progress curves indicate the development of an epidemic, as shown in figures 3 to 5. Pattern A is for a monocyclic disease (one life cycle of the pathogen in a growing season) with curves (a), (b) and (c) illustrating different rates of spread. Pattern B is for a typical polycyclic disease (such as potato blight) where there are several pathogen life cycles in a growing season, and Pattern C is for a bimodal polycyclic disease where, for example, blossom and fruit is separately affected by the same pathogen.

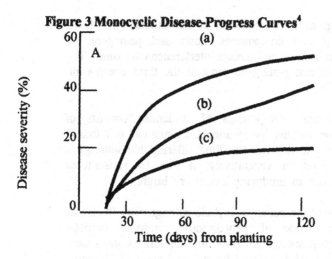

**Figure 3 Monocyclic Disease-Progress Curves[4]**

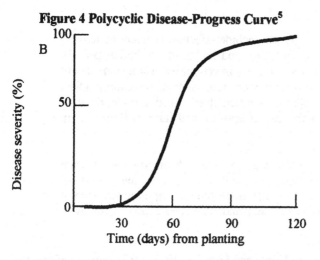

**Figure 4 Polycyclic Disease-Progress Curve[5]**

In anti-crop biological warfare, a monocyclic pattern with rapid spread (A(a)) has considerable potential, but a polycyclic pattern (B) with mass provision of initial inoculum, has even greater potential, because the deliberate provision of inoculum can establish the polycyclic infection early in the growing season.

**Figure 5  Bimodal Polycyclic Disease-Progress Curve[6]**

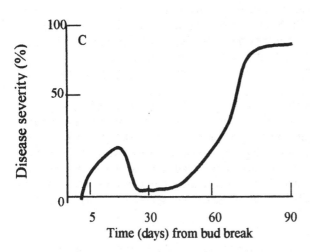

## 4. Discussion

The study of crop disease epidemiology has developed rapidly in the past 40 years, and the patterns of development of epidemics are well understood for most major diseases of the most significant food crops.   Experience of disease epidemics, often gained over many years, makes it possible to predict with some accuracy the likely development of endemic disease problems in any one growing season.

It is always possible to get sudden, unpredictable and  massive epidemics on particular crops, usually by virtue of a coincidence of crop susceptibility, a pathogen reservoir and the precisely necessary climatic conditions, but it is much more common to get a predictable spread of a disease.

Some of the greatest problems of crop losses have resulted from the spread of a pathogen to a region where it was not formerly present and where the crop varieties grown were notably susceptible to the pathogen.   It follows that this is one area where anti-crop biological warfare has potential, as does the deliberate production, by genetic modification, of a race (or races) of a pathogen intended to affect the specific varieties of a crop grown in a target state.

States are likely to be variably susceptible to anti-crop warfare depending on their levels and types of agricultural development.   A state with a highly developed agricultural research and extension service will have a certain capability to observe, predict and attempt to control unexpected epidemics, to the extent that the effects of an attack may be somewhat curtailed. This will be further aided if the crop under attack is either grown primarily on very large estates, or at least on relatively small numbers of large farms.

Crops such as sugarcane, cotton, tea and rubber may be grown on estates of over 10,000 acres, often with their own resident agronomy staff and with the crops monitored carefully on a weekly if not daily basis. Crops such as wheat, corn (maize) and soybean may be grown in some countries on many farms of over 1,000 acres each. Here again, knowledge of the unusual development of an epidemic can be communicated quickly to the relevant authorities and control measures attempted.

At the other end of the scale, states in which the majority of the population may be subsistence farmers will have crops grown in very large numbers of small plots scattered across the countryside, and often with many different varieties grown. There will frequently be intensive inter-cropping on individual plots, with any one plot combining the growing of root crops, bush crops, tall cereals and even climbers, mirroring a natural ecosystem. Apart from the ecological efficiency involved, such an agricultural pattern does serve substantially to hinder the spread of diseases, whether naturally occurring or induced.

A state which is most likely to be vulnerable to anti-crop biological warfare is a state which has system of arable agriculture which involve extensive mono-culture of important crops involving large numbers of small farms but does not have a well-developed research and extension service. In such a state, it will be less easy to detect an attack and there will not be the infrastructure required to respond with rapid control measures. Thus, states at a low or intermediate level of economic development are probably those most vulnerable to this form of warfare.

If anti-crop biological warfare is a serious concern for the future, and the evidence from the work of Whitby and others suggests that most of the major BW programmes to date have included anti-cop BW, then the minimum requirement is that should be widely recognised by the plant pathology community and more intensive work done on two aspects of the problem:

> a) researching more fully the most appropriate measures to distinguish
> naturally-occurring epidemics from induced epidemics, and

> b) strengthening the BTWC with respect to anti-crop biological
> warfare.

## 5. A Note on Sources

This paper is intended solely as an introductory summary of the subject of plant disease epidemics as they occur naturally, placed in the context of the potential for anti-crop biological warfare. It draws primarily and substantially on two standard plant pathology texts:

> George N. Agrios, *Plant Pathology*, third edition, Academic Press, 1988.

> J. G. Manners, *Principles of Plant Pathology*, Cambridge University Press, 1988.

## Notes

[1] Simon Whitby and Paul Rogers, "Anti-Crop Biological Warfare - Implications of the US and Iraqi Programmes", *Defense Analysis*, 13, 3, pp.303-318, 1997.

[2] Re-drawn from George N. Agrios, *Plant Pathology*, third edition, Academic Press, 1988.

[3] Re-drawn from J. G. Manners, *Principles of Plant Pathology*, Cambridge University Press, 1982

[4] Re-drawn from George N. Agrios, *op cit.*

[5] Re-drawn from *Ibid.*

[6] Re-drawn from *Ibid.*

# DISTINGUISHING NATURAL AND UNNATURAL OUTBREAKS OF ANIMAL DISEASES

MARTIN HUGH-JONES,
*Department of Epidemiology & Community Health,*
*School of Veterinary Medicine,*
*Louisiana State University,*
*Baton Rouge,*
*LA 70803, USA*

## 1. Introduction

This may be better reworded as "What is a suspicious (agricultural) incident?". Such a question by itself indicates that the cause of most such events are expected to be not immediately obvious.

Such agricultural incidents will differ significantly from those involving primarily targeting human beings as any human deaths will at worst be coincidental, even when zoonoses are concerned; any agricultural impact may be delayed significantly and only become obvious after weeks or even months; and the major losses follow from the disease and are not directly of the disease itself, which in comparison may be relatively trivial. An effective 'attack' does not necessitate massive death and destruction, quite the reverse. It is the necessary responses to agricultural disease, to contain and clean up, to prevent further spread, and then to reclaim the previous level of disease control or freedom, lost exports, and international recognition that eat up effort and funding. There is a very different time scale and series of available tools than those involving public health and human BW. The desired results from an agricultural BW attack are much more complicated than the simple widespread terror induced in a human target population.

Such an agricultural incident will have the following characteristics:

> The event itself:
> 1.1: Unusual time &/or place, i.e. at extremes of normal distribution;
> &/or
> 1.2: Unexpected strain of agent, or multiple strains;
> &/or
> 1.3: Marked reversal of an otherwise steady progress in disease control or freedom;
> &/or
> 1.4: Epidemiologically "Weird" event ... it in no way matches normal experience or knowledge.

*M. Dando et al. (eds.),*
*Scientific and Technical Means of Distinguishing Between Natural and Other Outbreaks of Disease, 63–73.*
© 2001 *Kluwer Academic Publishers.*

Directly resulting in:

2.1: Marked economic or political costs with benefits, possibly singular, to a competitor;

&/or

2.2: Removal of target country/industry from international trade;

&/or

2.3: Target country must continue imports from competitor;

&/or

2.4: Marked social unrest, maybe with the movement of a significant part of the population as a result of losing their livestock or crops.

While the above would be expected in all circumstances, even when allowing for the "&/or"s, there may be additional and suggestive aspects.

Additional weighting:

3.1: Diagnosis ... unusual circumstances;

3.2: Publicity ... premature or from obscure source(s);

3.3: Coded claim(s) of authorship;

3.4: Echoes or previous or subsequent events.

These will be discussed in greater detail in Section (3). It should be kept in mind that it is hard to envisage any circumstances in which a country or commercial company would publicly claim or admit to have been involved in active BW against another. The public and global opprobrium would be damning. But this is not to mean that blame for such an event, real or imagined, would not be stage managed to be laid at another's door. Disinformation on a perfectly normal outbreak — much less one that has been contrived — could be so structured as to be persuasive and withstand nominal investigation. The reality is surely that there will be more disinformation put out than actual agricultural BW attacks mounted.

## 2. Application to Interpretation of Future Incidents

There is a need to have done one's 'homework' well before any future incidents, both to give a frame of reference and provide a body of updatable knowledge, but also to save time when it happens. If and when such an 'incident' should occur there is certain to be some institutional panic and reactive demands that "something must be done". Maybe not. But when a decision is made to follow up such an incident the response should move with deliberate speed.

Target pre-identification:

1.1: Define hypothetical "goals" of potential attackers;

1.2: Identify their probable objectives and rank them;

1.3: Prioritise critical target-countries, and industries;

1.4: Follow up with preparatory collection of data and confirmation of the existence of a minimal administrative / organisational infrastructure within each target-country or industry; identify liaison persons/local guides in case of need;

1.5: Ensure that reference databases of strain characteristics already exist and are readily accessible — there is no point in having to do these comparison analyses on top of the urgent field samples.

Early warning indicators:

2.1: Develop systems to warn of possible incipient attacks;

2.1.1: Normal intelligence awareness activities;

2.1.2: Monitor for "Own-goals" — telltale accidents within a notional 'attacker' country or commercial company, maybe in relation to known institutes, or outside the country and well away from target crops or livestock;

2.1.3: Sentinel or "canary" animals/flocks and unexpected minor events — "Hang-fires" — possible unsuccessful attacks with only a few cases;

2.1.4: Travellers at airports found with cultures, with or without adequate explanations;

2.2: If the above apply, go to stand-by alert.

Prepared response:

3.1: Have appropriate game plan(s) agreed and ready before it is needed;

3.2: Limit response to initial events and the identification of first isolates;

3.3: Plan to get people into the field quickly to collect and archive information and samples, with initial processing of samples in the field;

3.4: Ensure that they can maintain a strict, fully documented audit trail on all materials collected, whether or not analysed, in case of the need for later recommendations.

# 3. Identification of Methods for the Analyst to use in Assessing Suspicious Outbreaks Involving Agriculture and Other Applicable Cases, Including Economic Cost Incurred

One must always be aware that BW events will be rare and therefore any suspicious incident is most likely to have a normal if not prosaic explanation whatever the initial impression or belief. Similarly, the implications of a proven attack are so far reaching that any investigation resulting in such a conclusion must be so thorough as to survive the most rigorous of examinations. Therefore, unless the circumstances are blatantly those of an obvious BW event — the biological equivalent of the recent Oklahoma bombing, for example — ten widely separated cases of rinderpest across the USA within one week — the primary investigative position is that the situation was normal and, if unexpected, merely unusual. Thus Rule One: Rule out normality. And Rule Two: Try harder to rule out normality. Only if that fails does Rule Three apply: 'Round up all the usual suspects.'

## 3.1 EPIDEMIOLOGICAL INVESTIGATION

Based on informed epidemiological experience, literature, and databases, 99/100 such outbreaks will be normal events and fully explicable from existing knowledge. Events at the extremes of normal probabilities are by their nature infrequent but not *ipso facto* abnormal. An event having a low probability will only acquire persuasion when matched or unmatched with other events. 'Experience' may indicate that certain infrequent events are commonly associated with a specific set of circumstances and these may be missing in a contrived and not-normal outbreak. Therefore the events leading up to the 'incident' must be carefully analysed by experienced investigators.

Investigations should also cover commercial legal and illegal importations of likely fomites (e.g., machinery, used sacks, harness), vaccines, vectors, fruits, seed, birds and poultry, eggs, livestock and livestock feed & feed components.

## 3.2 STRAIN IDENTIFICATION

Isolates from the initial outbreaks should be compared rapidly with known isolates in the pathogen archives. The molecular & PCR structure based on **standardised** techniques should be compared with the library of known markers and sequences.

* With luck and a comprehensive collection, it may exactly match a known strain with a documented origin.

* If 'new', it might lie within a group of known regional or national origin.

* With a measurable variation it may be possible to place it both in a general area and within a geographical radius of one or radii of other known strains.

* The genomic markers may be associated with a specific ecology and/or host species, further defining its natural origin.

* If multiple strains are identified, are they logical? Do they have any other characteristics, such as resistance to a number of antibiotics, a documented collective availability to one institute, or an unusual common ability such as to successfully withstand freeze-drying while others commonly do not? If they are very diverse, their likelihood of naturally occurring together must be regarded as remote, at least until other evidence is available.

* But Country "A" in 'attacking' Country "B" may use strains or vectors from Country "C". Therefore just because the identified strain is associated with one origin does not mean with certainty that it came directly from there.

* Are the possible "attacker(s)" or their contractees capable technically and scientifically of effectively mounting such an offence ... Is there documented expertise, travel in area, and documented ownership of or access to the identified strain(s).

The results of any successful strain identification must be promptly transmitted to the investigation team as it may open up a series of new questions and probabilities.

## 3.3 EXISTING CONTROL PROGRAMMES

Carefully and objectively investigate situation and existing programme's surveillance system. The set-back to the programme is probably 100% expectable in hindsight, especially if the outbreak has revealed imbedded defects in the programme design, implementation, reporting cycle and response time, funding, training, or tactical control. Many national disease control programmes work well until they are challenged by a real epidemic; cf. Taiwan and the recent FMD epidemic, which appears to have originated in some smuggled viraemic pigs from mainland China and then probably exacerbated by the new owners selling ill pigs into the market system. Similarly, the present anti-rinderpest campaign in Africa could have a set-back either because of local inefficiencies or because of purposeful interference.

However, a new case in an area well cleared of disease for a number of years and with farmers experienced and knowledgeable of the costs to be incurred if the condition were to be reintroduced must get one's attention. But farmer cupidity is not unknown, just as is their ability to be seduced by cheap animals with dodgey paperwork. Local knowledge is a significant help in sorting out such scenarios as well as in interviewing the affected farmers.

One should never lose sight of the possibility of unexpected outbreaks following upon the illegal importation of fruit and livestock, which by definition lack the appropriate certificates and health guarantees. These will generally follow a pattern of expectations of those knowledgeable in fighting these risks — medfly in fruit from Central America, tubercular cattle across the Texas-Mexico border, smuggled parrots and Newcastle disease, and drugs associated events. What characterises these events is that there are no external beneficiaries other than those individuals directly involved in the illegal activities.

## 3.4 INEXPLICABLE EVENTS

These are "weird" events that go far beyond expectations, such as VEE in Switzerland; vector borne diseases in areas without appropriate vectors; normally feed-borne diseases in stock not receiving feed; outbreaks on isolated farms or ranches, from which for a number of years animals had only been sold, not bought in. Was the spread of outbreaks in line with existing knowledge and was it independent of normal commercial / industrial activities, marketing, weather, and/or livestock/crop densities? For example, if the infection is normally windborne (e.g., with certain FMDV) was the initial disease spread downwind or across the prevailing wind direction; if it is density dependent, such as with bovine brucellosis, was it first noted in one or more small herds with less than ten cows? Was the outbreak in the dry season while the local vectors are all wet-season breeders?

In brief, the outbreak does not make epidemiological sense. It is totally outside normal experience or knowledge. Obviously, this might still be a natural outbreak, amply providing a new and unappreciated insight into the disease, and must be investigated in case this is so. Even the ten rinderpest cases, mentioned earlier, might be explainable if it were found to be related to a recent importation of Wildebeest from Africa that somehow were cleared from quarantine early and shipped to widely dispersed "Wildlife" parks with resident beef cattle or nearby dairy farms.

## 3.5 ECONOMIC AND TRADE ANALYSIS

Under normal circumstances all countries will try to take advantage of another country's problems whatever their cause. So judgement here has a large measure of subjectivity unless taken in regard to the previous "Event Characteristics".

There must be a concordance between the goals and objectives of a suspect Organization and the suspicious BW event; e.g., The United Fruit Company might well want to bankrupt the banana export industry in the Lesser Antilles but this would not be achieved through an outbreak of FMD in pigs in Castries, St Lucia.

A careful analysis must be made of whether the first three 'direct' results (2.1, 2.2, and 2.3) have been successfully achieved and to what degree did which countries benefit: e.g., if Country "B" suffers an outbreak, which countries increased — or against expectations did not decrease — their trade in the same period. And if so, by how much did they benefit from "B"s problems. Or on the other hand in a notional prospective analysis, how much would they benefit? Nationally the lost of exports will reverberate back reducing national demand and thereby producing excesses which can be very expensive to absorb.

## 3.6 'BANK-SHOT' SCENARIOS

1. The C.I.S. improves its infrastructure and will soon be self-sufficient in wheat. Argentina uses USA rust spores against the C.I.S. C.I.S. accuses the USA and cuts off US imports of grain, and probably much else. Argentina increases its grain exports to the C.I.S., along with other benefiting countries.

2. China releases rust spores in the Ukraine, thereby reducing the latter's harvest and capability of exporting grain to the C.I.S.. China increases its exports to the

C.I.S.Ukraine now cannot cover energy requirements and becomes politically unstable, thereby deflecting C.I.S. attention to its Ukrainian border, and away from China.

## 3.7 PEOPLE MOVEMENTS

Social unrest will aid terrorism and the latter's desire for political anarchy, opportunity, power, and change or refusal to change. At sporadic levels agricultural BW events will produce uncertainty and increased tension. At its most extreme in an agricultural economy when one kills the livestock and markedly reduces harvests the people must move if they are to survive. Thus it may also provide a land vacuum attracting third parties. The latter situation played a significant part in the civil wars in the former Yugoslavia.

In the Ethiopian war with Somalia, Somalis living in the Ogaden had their livestock attacked with the result that the people had to take refuge with their relatives in Somalia. The influx of refugees, with some of their livestock, especially small ruminants, overloaded the governing capacity of the Somali government as well as accelerating over-grazing and desertification of various family and clan seasonal grazing areas.

The original "Yellow Rain" incident was perceived by many was being a direct attack on the Hmung hill peoples though the cutaneous human disease rate was not always significant. What was consistent was the devastation inflicted on their ducks, chickens, pigs and cattle. Trichothecene mycotoxins are a significant pathogen for these animals, who were thus clearly the target. It can be argued, with some force, that by attacking their food and livestock the strategy was to force the Hmung out of the hills and down into the lowland controlled Laotian villages.

These events would be characterised by repetition and gross direct losses. In general one would expect that they would lack the sophistication of attacks on developed and intensive agricultural systems.

## 3.8 DIAGNOSIS

Most agricultural costs from outbreaks are self-inflicted by the host country in responding to the outbreak and the need for rapid resolution. This is usually out of all proportion to the number of index or primary cases. Therefore the 'initial' hit can be singular, even numerically trivial (e.g., Botswana with one FMD case; Israel and $HgCl_2$ in an orange; Chile and half a box of grapes). Under these circumstances the "attacker" must aid the diagnostic process to ensure that the instance is (1) recognised and (2) reported. Therefore, what were the circumstances leading up to the initial recognition of the incident and its subsequent diagnosis and laboratory confirmation?

Similarly, had the surveillance and diagnostic capacities been recently improved? Therefore, could it have been a normal case that would otherwise have been missed? E.g., diagnosis of endemic cholera via naturally contaminated Blue crabs in southern

Louisiana is function of physician awareness and laboratory enthusiasm. Outbreaks of human cholera follow upon hot, drier than usual summers, and the Cajun preference for not over-cooking their seafood. One successful diagnosis will beget others and soon there may be an unexpected "epidemic", a loss of tourists, and the refusal of other states to buy Louisiana Blue crabs (which might otherwise have been relabelled as "Chesapeake Bay Blue Crabs"), and all it was was a hot, dry summer.

Therefore, one should always be aware of personnel competence, training, and technical laboratory improvements on surveillance efficiency.

## 3.9 PUBLICITY

Most conditions have to be reported under various statutory orders and circumstances to OIE, FAO, WHO, etc, quite apart from national regulations. International reporting is frequently either monthly or annually; only a limited number must be reported immediately. Did it get reported "too quickly" and what were the circumstances? Latterly one sees instances where cases of human CJD get reported in the local US newspapers as "Mad Cow Disease", sometimes with immediate effect on beef futures prices. This is just journalistic ignorance and stupidity but it could equally well be purposeful in the appropriate circumstances. With the internet, CNN, ProMED-mail, and modern information systems the opportunities for rapid, global dissemination of news is almost unlimited.

Within ProMED-mail we have already begun to see instances of "stirring", of certain individuals regularly referring local news reports in distant cities that reflect very specific personal viewpoints. While it would be naive to think that this was in any way new but the global internet facilitates it for more people who would not otherwise be in 'news' dissemination.

There are other advantages in keeping the reporting of disease outbreaks to the routine, usual procedure. One can then watch for "premature" reports and take appropriate investigative action when they are noted.

## 3.10 CODED CLAIMS OF AUTHORSHIP

The only groups that would admit to initiating a BW attack on agriculture, when not in wartime, would be terrorists. No country or commercial company would wish to. Such terrorist claims would reflect a grab for power, to increase social unrest, or for market share in mercenary activities.

There will be frequent false claims.

## 3.11 ECHOES

BW events do not occur in isolation. A successful 'attack' will follow successful research and field trials. Similarly, it is unlikely that a successfully completed 'attack' will not be repeated, i.e. be a 'one-off'. Any technology has a parenthood and genealogy attached to it; for example, similar research will be reported in different institutes by students of the originators; scientists are surprising unoriginal sometimes so that trials get repeated and mimicked by other groups. So any event has the capacity to cast a 'shadow' forward and backwards in time. Thus a BW-suspect event without such echoes or shadows may well not be BW related.

## 4. Application of these Pointers to the 1973 Newcastle Disease Outbreak in Northern Ireland

The event itself: Certainly unexpected as Northern Ireland did not and does not import animal proteins or by-products, such as bone meals or poultry offal meals. In retrospect probably from a contamination of a European feed grains by the then Western European pandemic strain. While there were 15 feed-compounder mills involved, importation was via only two agents. All the initial isolates were identical except for the "known" over-vaccination related outbreak.

Directly resulting in: An economic cost of £668,994 (or £4.7m to £5.1m in 1997 terms) but the benefits were diffuse as the province returned to full production quickly. Most countries in Europe had Newcastle disease problems at that time which would have limited their trading capacity. The demand for table eggs was declining rapidly in the UK. In reality there was slight benefit to anyone outside Northern Ireland in this outbreak. There were no obvious social or political impacts inside the country. In fact the outbreak brought all those involved closer together.

Additional aspects: None, which is indicative of a non-BW but natural, though unknown, source.

Of course, if viewed from the opposite direction varied NDV strains would be characteristic of an aggressive group with tight security and three separate teams, each with their own infected eggs to be placed broken in the targeted flocks so that they would be eaten by the chickens; or however else delivery was to be achieved. A Roswell interpretation in the opinion of the writer in the absence of any strategic advantage.

## 5. Recommendations for Identifying &/or Avoiding Future Incidents, Minimising Economic Damage, and Containing the Disease

This can only be covered briefly here in this report as there are thick books of government regulations and standard procedures to cover the control and eradication of most agricultural diseases likely to be used for BW. And such clean-up activities come under the proper purview of government veterinary services. The following brief suggestions are to reduce overall costs and to reduce any public hysteria and political over-reaction that might be engendered by a successful agricultural BW attack.

* Develop *early warning* indicators.

* Define hypothetical goals and possible objectives of those likely to use agricultural BW techniques.

* The more developed the industry, the more likely that the target component will be exports via singular cases (e.g., in reaction to the diagnosis of a BSE-like case in the USA): similarly, the less developed, the more likely that it will involve cruder processes and large numbers (e.g., "yellow rain", rinderpest).

* Any preferred technique will involve a high impact:effort ratio; i.e. small effort with large impact.

* Be prepared without being paranoid; maintain an attitude of "informed suspicion".

* Have reliable rapid diagnostic tests released to the general agricultural community so as to reduce the frequency of false alarms.

* Dual applicability of DNA test kits.

* Strengthen laboratory systems in the regions identified at risk.

* Maintain field investigation team expertise and abilities. Try not to replace each *ad hoc* team with yet another. Better to rotate individuals in & out, not teams.

The political temptation is to suppress notification of disease outbreaks. It is better to be proactive with the news thereby having some control of it and also insuring that it is accurate. Hiding information is a good way of ensuring that it is discovered and trumpeted without warning. Better to facilitate accurate news in a low-key manner than to suppress it. However because of the implications — a true BW attack is an act of war — it is wise to not inform the news agencies of the BW nature of the suspected or confirmed source. That should be left to those responsible for national policy. Because of the risk of imitation by others, revealing a successful terrorist attack as BW may be counter-indicated.

* On the other hand there is much to be said for not publicising "near-misses" and "hang-fires". Firstly, as any publicity would engender unnecessary excitement and speculation; secondly, watch to see what happens and note accordingly.

* Preplan the agricultural, economic, & policy response. If necessary, publicise one's intentions. Minimise self-inflicted economic wounds. The recovery must be rapid.

* Preplan tactics and operations, including legislation, for carcass/crop disposal, site disinfection, and compensation. Compensation at market value paid promptly will significantly reduce delays in reporting suspect animals/crops and reinforce community support.

* Run field "war games" so that government staff and representatives of the professional public are rehearsed. These should not be overtly "anti-BW" but a routine "What do we do if there is an outbreak of FMD/VEE/ND/whatever". They have drills for hurricanes and tornadoes, why not for agricultural emergencies? Reduce the potential for hysteria by widening the range of those involved. With each year there is an increasing need to be prepared and rehearsed.

* If it is appropriate, maintain basic stocks of vaccines. While, for example, outbreaks of anthrax can be readily and efficiently stopped by vaccination, for other diseases (e.g., FMD) it may be better to slaughter one's way out of them because of the knock-on effects of vaccination on international recognition of being disease free. It depends on circumstances.

# DETECTING ANTHRAX: WHAT WE LEARNED FROM THE 1979 SVERDLOVSK OUTBREAK

JEANNE GUILLEMIN
*Department of Sociology*
*Boston College*
*Boston*
*United States*

## 1. Introduction

The 1979 outbreak in Sverdlovsk, USSR, is the largest and only example of a local community victimised by inhalation anthrax. In retrospect the incident supports concern that distinctions between natural and manufactured causes of such outbreaks are difficult to draw. The official Soviet explanation that the cause was anthrax infected meat was plausible until the facts of the disaster were better known. Although the disaster was likely accidental, its occurrence and consequences sufficiently mimic a terrorist or state assault on citizens for us to appreciate it as a model of attack and civic response. What have we learned about the Sverdlovsk outbreak that would be useful in both discerning and managing a similar BW scenario? Before addressing this question, I will review the sources of our data for composing the two maps that were published in the November 18, 1994 issue of *Science.*[1] Then I will describe the data on onset, hospital admission, and death rates as possible clues to what can be done to identify an outbreak, provided, of course, the political will is there to investigate.

## 2. Sources of Data

*Interviews* were the most important and extensive source of information for discovering the daytime locations of victims of the anthrax outbreak during the first week of April, 1979, locations on which the map of the anthrax plume is based. *Documents* were also crucial, three in particular: the KGB list of victims, veterinary records of livestock deaths, and meteorologic information from the local airport and weather stations. Of the 68 people on the final Soviet list, I and my three Russian colleagues (Ilona Popova, Irina Belaeva, and Olga Yampolskaya) were able to locate the families or friends of 55, and also to interview 10 survivors. The key was to find the position in space and time that all the victims shared prior to falling ill. In addition, I was able to interview individuals from five households in the village of Abramovo, southeast of Sverdlovsk, whose animals had died of anthrax beginning April 5, 1979. These interviews confirmed that the plume had traversed the city boundary and, with diminishing lethality, affected livestock in the countryside.

*M. Dando et al. (eds.),*
*Scientific and Technical Means of Distinguishing Between Natural and Other Outbreaks of Disease, 75–85.*
© 2001 *Kluwer Academic Publishers.*

Other documents, some fragmentary, were an important means of cross checking the interview data. The 42 hand-written autopsy case notes of Dr. Faina Abramova, the pathologist in charge in 1979, lists of patients from a community hospital, the hospital records of five survivors, and death certificates held by private individuals helped compensate for the nearly total lack of hospital and public health records, which were apprehended by the central government in 1979 and not available to us. Information from Soviet officials included a generally accurate graph of the victims' death dates, but no other evidence of epidemiologic inquiry. We also cross-checked names and dates on cemetery markers with other identifying sources.

*Medical Science* was another important source of information about the 1979 anthrax outbreak. Patho-anatomical samples from 42 cases analysed by Dr. Abramova and Dr. Lev Grinberg provided independent confirmation that the outbreak was indeed anthrax and probably inhalational.[2] Their testimony and the testimony of other physicians confirmed that the first bacteriological report that the disease was anthrax came on April 11, 1979.

Map No.1 (in the 1994 *Science* article[1]) illustrated that on the afternoon of April 2, 1979 an anthrax plume traversed the Chkalovsky ward (*rayon*) in a southeasterly direction. It originated at Military Compound 19, passed through the eastern edge of Compound 32 and into a residential district of small cottages and several apartment buildings. Directly in its path was a large ceramics factory (in the marked rectangle), beyond which were other industrial workplaces.

Map No.2 (in the 1994 *Science* article[1]) illustrated the extension of the plume into the countryside. The circle labelled F is the village of Abramovo, 50 kilometres southeast of Sverdlovsk. The Soviet claim that anthrax was endemic in this rural area was historically credible. Yet in the tainted meat explanation, a specific contamination of feed and a resulting epizootic was said to have occurred in March, prior to the epidemic. The official understanding seemed to be that human deaths began in early April and lasted into May as infected meat continued to be consumed. Interviews with villagers and verification of veterinary records placed the earliest animal deaths at April 5, after the April 2 emission.

## 3. Onset, Admission, and Mortality Data

Our understanding of the 1979 outbreak is much fuller than these maps represent. In my questionnaire I asked respondents to narrate the onset of the victim's symptoms and then tell me about the medical response. When possible, this account was cross-checked with autopsy notes and hospital records and found to be highly reliable with regard to both symptoms and dates.

3.1 ONSET

Onset (figure 1) of symptoms were recorded as early as April 4 and as late as May 15. A dozen or so patients exhibited the early, influenza-like symptoms that seemed to diminish in a day, only to be followed by more severe symptoms (high fever, fainting, difficulty breathing, extreme nausea and vomiting).

**Figure 1. Onset**

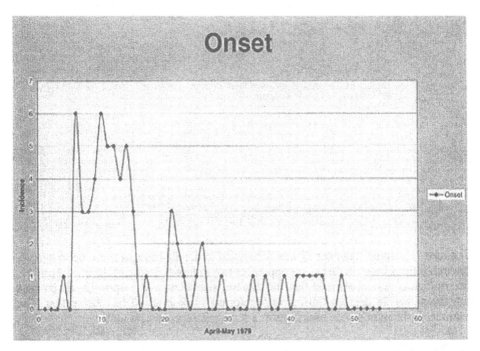

At least six victims had their early symptoms dismissed by physicians as not serious. More commonly, patients were overwhelmed by the disease. They may have stoically denied earlier symptoms. In any event, nearly a week passed after the emission of the anthrax spores before the outbreak was discernible. It was 9 days before laboratory confirmation of anthrax was obtained.

3.2 ADMISSIONS

Admissions (figure 2), by April 9-10 the infectious disease division of a large hospital (number 40) had been designated as the referral treatment Center, particularly from the two ward hospitals (Numbers 20 and 24).

**Figure 2. Hospital Admission**

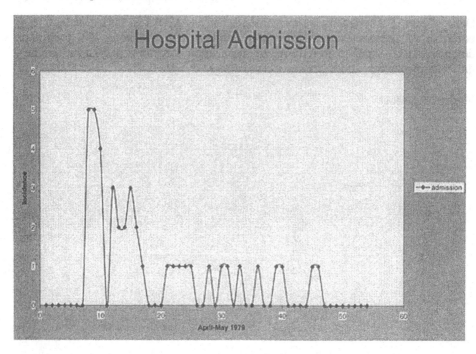

A children's hospital (Number 3) was designated to handle cases of those up to age 14, although serious cases in this age group never materialised. By the evening of April 11, bacteriological tests confirmed that the disease was anthrax. By April 12, all patients with fever over 38 degrees Celsius were referred to Hospital 40 for observation. The treatment of the most severe cases was in a segregated special care unit.

## 3.3 DEATHS

Deaths (figure 3) during the outbreak signalled a disaster had occurred. The first recorded deaths were at local hospitals on April 8-9. Most deaths occurred within two days of the onset of severe symptoms. Despite a rapid public health response, good communication between hospitals, emergency ambulance services on alert, and the screening of hundreds of patients, 14 people died at home or on the street (4 at home on the 10-12 April, 4 at home and 2 on the street between 14-18 April). By April 12, when the laboratory test confirmation of anthrax was broadcast to hospitals, 21 people had already died. Animal deaths verified as anthrax occurred from April 5-9 onward. Other sheep and cattle deaths were reported for earlier dates but lacked laboratory confirmation of anthrax.

**Figure 3. Deaths**

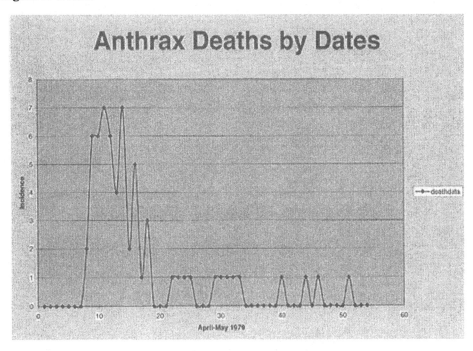

## Anthrax Deaths by Dates

### 3.4 TEMPORAL PROFILE OF THE OUTBREAK

Combined Data on Onset, Admission, and Death (figure 4) illustrates the temporal profile of the outbreak. Its worst phase was undoubtedly April 7 to April 18, after which fatalities diminished. The duration of the epidemic was technically until the last death, at home, on May 21. This protracted time line was a source of confusion on all sides. The presumption was made (and is still sometimes made in the press) that a single lethal emission of anthrax would kill all victims quickly. From the Soviet perspective, protracted duration of the outbreak, along with the area's history of animal outbreaks, substantiated the tainted meat explanation. Ignored was the 1956 monkey research by D.H. Henderson that clearly pointed out the possibility for lethal spores to remain dormant in the lungs for weeks, even months after exposure to aerosolised anthrax.[3]

Figure 4. Combined Data on Onset, Admissions and Deaths

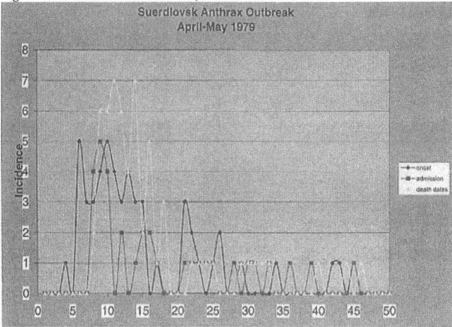

Figure 5. Deaths by Age and Sex

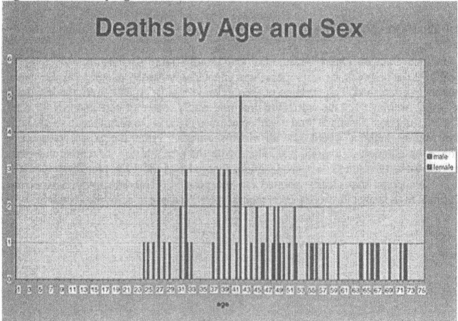

## 3.5 AGE AND SEX DISTRIBUTION

Age and Sex Distribution of Victims (figure 5) tells us about individual susceptibility. At its finish, the anthrax outbreak had no mortal effect on children or young people under the age of 24. Despite rumours that it was a special strain invented to kill men of military age, the epidemic was especially lethal for older people. Of the 66 cases for which we have death dates, 52 people were over age 37, half were age 45 or over. This age distribution suggests that compromised immune systems made these victims more susceptible to anthrax than the general population. Women were approximately one-quarter of the victims, with a median age of 54.

Except for a schoolteacher who was 24, the other 17 women were 32 and older, with an average age of 56. Relative to women, men are commonly over represented in epidemics because of differences in their immune systems. In the older age grades, men tend to be under represented because of decreased life expectancy. This is especially so in the former Soviet Union, where the Second World War reduced the population of men who in 1979 were over 52.

## 4. Public Health Organization

The 1979 Sverdlovsk medical and public health response was on five levels: the micro-rayon, the rayon, the city, the oblast, and the central government in Moscow. After April 12 and certainly by April 15, special committees at the city and local levels had ceded their authority to Moscow. Local-level administrators organised community-level brigades of factory worker volunteers and physicians that did house checks, distributed antibiotics to households of victims, disinfected homes, took meat samples, washed buildings, paved streets, and administered a vaccination program for nearly 50,000 people. None of these efforts spoke to the problem of a single causality, nor was there open questioning about the source of the anthrax infection.

The circumstances for containing the outbreak were optimal. Everyone spoke the same language and was familiar with the medical system. The physician-patient ratio was high and the population was geographically stable. Although initially families and medical personnel panicked (before it was understood the disease was not contagious human-to-human), the consensus was high that the medical and public health response was adequate. Families in the village of Abramovo, which was quarantined for about a month, were distinctly unhappy with the loss of livestock, destruction of outbuildings, forced vaccinations and other inconveniences they endured. Though fearful, the afflicted population in general was amenable to a variety of public health responses to the outbreak. One in particular violated local custom, the return of the deceased's body to the family for washing and dressing for burial. Instead, the bodies of victims were sealed with lime in closed coffins and buried in a separate section of one of the city cemeteries.

## 5. Investigating Anthrax

One important lesson from the Sverdlovsk outbreak investigation is that data sources have to be local and they have to be cross-checked. From this lesson it follows that sites have to be open to investigations with methods of inquiry that are multi-dimensional.

### 5.1 SURVEYS

An epidemiologic survey is not always easy to implement nor are crucial documents necessarily available. Access to surviving victims and to their families, friends, and community is crucial and the obstacles to free access are many. One obstacle is at the level of government. Investigation would have been impossible in the Sverdlovsk of 1979 due to central government restrictions. In other contexts, access to the names and addresses of victims requires either government or hospital staff cooperation and, from an ethical perspective, the consent of individuals.

The timing of an investigation can be crucial. Even if a government has the political will to discover the source of an outbreak, the fact that an outbreak has taken place may not be understood for days. Confusion about early anthrax symptoms is predictable. If medical and public health personnel are less than careful in record-keeping, valuable information can be lost.

A community's reaction to an outbreak can be an obstacle to data gathering. A less oppressed population than the one in Sverdlovsk might panic or bolt. So might medical personnel. Europeans who fled to the hinterlands to escape the Black Plague four hundred years ago would find kindred spirits in any similar outbreak today. Or cultural forces might foster resistance to cooperation. Russians might be willing to talk about the loss of a relative or friend, but some traditions disallow speaking of the dead. Gender role is no small factor in conducting interviews. In some cultures, male strangers are not supposed to speak to women in or outside their homes. In others, even a professional woman would have difficulty asking questions of men. Language and dialect can be serious obstacles. No outside team should investigate without either training in the local language and culture or enough qualified interpreters to facilitate communication.

It remains a question, then, whether outside investigators can or should intrude locally when an epidemic is at its height and if much is to be gained by quick access. By the end of May, 1979, when the anthrax outbreak was over, the vaccination program well underway, and the quarantine lifted on the southeastern villages, investigators might have promptly located the source of the outbreak. But knowing about this appropriate timing would have been dependent on local contacts with good judgement.

### 5.2 LABORATORY RESULTS

Results. In the 1979 anthrax outbreak, unfortunately, the recognition that an anthrax outbreak was happening did not dawn until almost a third of the victims had died. Even then, the distinction that the portal of entry was the lungs and not the intestines was not known. Modern laboratory analysis in most countries has a potential for much swifter returns now than in 1979 in Sverdlovsk. But even sophisticated tests cannot distinguish between inhalation and intestinal anthrax, which can be difficult even at autopsy. At best, anthrax might be quickly distinguished from influenza, pneumonia, or bronchitis. But then it would be necessary to start reckoning the numbers of victims through case screening, which was well done in Sverdlovsk, and tracking when and where they were exposed, which was not done at all.

## 6. Laying the Groundwork for Investigation

The most important strategy for BW investigations that can be worked out in advance is to lay the groundwork for international cooperation. The kinds of data that were invaluable for uncovering the source of the 1979 anthrax outbreak in Sverdlovsk (interviews, documents, and medical science) maintain their importance. But the framework for a like investigation has broadened beyond the old boundaries. Covert weapons activities are much harder to conceal within a national defense or security structure, especially where weapons of mass destruction are concerned. The global political will, manifest in treaties, is for transparency. So, too, is the impetus of information technologies which heighten international communication among individuals.

### 6.1 INTERNATIONAL COLLEAGUES

If outsiders to the locale are commissioned to investigate (which is often the case for important natural outbreaks), it is better if the means of access to the locale is laid down in advance. Our entry into Yekaterinburg depended on international academic contacts that long antedated our first trip in 1992. An established scientist, Matthew Meselson, the leader of the research team in 1992 and a persistent advocate for getting to the facts about the 1979 anthrax outbreak, was able to open doors for us that, even in the "new Russia" of 1992, would have been shut. Our host in Yekaterinburg was the Urals State University. Our own investigation on the 1979 outbreak would have been impossible without academic colleagues in Yekaterinburg working alongside us. The approach via colleagues is hardly foolproof. National loyalties can and do override professional contacts. The suggestion here is that the options for access to foreign locales are greater in proportion to international scientific ties we can cultivate.

### 6.2 MONITORING NATURAL OCCURRENCES

Understanding a deviant event is impossible unless the patterns of natural disease outbreaks are understood. Those patterns may obfuscate a laboratory accident, as we learned from the Sverdlovsk outbreak, or mask a planned attack. Still, a better knowledge base is the only answer to questions about the numbers of human victims affected (whether it fits a reasonable range), the symptoms they present, and the circumstances surrounding any concurrent epizootic, if there has been one. The present global monitoring of natural anthrax epidemics and other outbreaks is a great advantage over previous times. Not only high speed information technology is helping this enterprise, but the concerted cooperation of local individuals and institutions with global entities like the World Health Organization is proving vital.[4] The more local-level the verification of specific outbreaks, the better.

## 6.3 MEDICAL RESEARCH ON ANTHRAX

Prevention and treatment issues are far from resolved for inhalation anthrax. That virtually no young people or children were affected by the 1979 anthrax outbreak in Sverdlovsk indicates that we have much to learn about the role of the immune system as it affects susceptibility to the disease. Hundreds of woolen mill workers in the last century and this were exposed to anthrax spores but showed no clinical symptoms. Who, then, is at greatest risk for inhalation anthrax?

What should be the prophylactic treatment of exposure to inhalation anthrax? The long duration of the 1979 outbreak reminds us that anthrax spores have the capacity to remain dormant within the lungs. We do not know the effect of the distribution of antibiotics in the area beneath the plume, but the number of later cases might have been reduced by it. Ceramics workers, for example, were at high risk of exposure. Yet only around 2% succumbed. Was it that they were members of families that were given antibiotics or that they had better immune systems? Even after 20 years, it remains possible to investigate that question and others concerning the consequences of exposure.

Who should be vaccinated and with what vaccine? The U.S. military program for anthrax vaccinations has already begun, but have we the best scientific basis for understanding what vaccines can or ought to do? New research on the paradoxical role of macrophages in both fighting and promoting infections[5] suggests an especially productive avenue of science research. Certainly this one and other inquiries involving vaccine development can foster cooperative U.S.-Russian programs that are post-Cold War models of transparency. The integration of Compound 19's laboratory into a joint program would go far to dispel the metaphorical cloud that still lingers over that facility.

## Notes

[1]  Matthew Meselson, Jeanne Guillemin, Martin Hugh-Jones et al. "The Sverdlovsk Anthrax Outbreak of 1979" *Science*, 266: 5188, 18 November 1994.

[2]  F.A. Abramova, L.M. Grinberg, O.V. Yampolskaya, D.H. Walker "Pathology of Inhalational Anthrax in 42 Cases from the Sverdlovsk Outbreak in 1979" *Proceedings of the National Academy of Science, U.S.A.*, 90, 2291-2294, 1993.

[3]  D.W. Henderson, S. Peacock, and F.C. Belton "Observations on the Prophylaxis of Experimental Pulmonary Anthrax in the Monkey" *Journal of Hygiene*, 54, 28-36.

[4]  Bradford A. Kay, Ralph J. Timperi, Stephen S. Morse et al. "Innovative Information-Sharing Strategies" *Emerging Infectious Diseases*, 4: 3, July-September 1998, 465-466.

[5] See, for example, the exchange between Philip Hanna and Nicholas Duesbury "How Anthrax Kills" *Science,* 280, 12 June 1998, 1671-1674.

# SCIENTIFIC TECHNIQUES TO DISTINGUISH NATURAL AND OTHER OUTBREAKS OF DISEASE

BEN STEYN
*Special Advisor to the Surgeon General*
*South African Defence Forces*
*Wierda Park*
*South Africa*

## 1. Introduction

Outbreaks of diseases are common natural occurrences all over the world and public health authorities on all levels spend much time on the detection and investigation of such outbreaks. Most unusual disease outbreaks are of natural origin and will be confirmed as such, i.e. a natural, though unusual outbreak.

The differentiation between these occurrences and the few cases where an unusual outbreak might not be of natural origin do pose a complicated problem which can only be addressed by proper investigation by highly qualified experts with the proper support.

### 1.1 DEFINITIONS

*An Outbreak of Disease (epidemic)*
An unusual outbreak of disease (epidemic) is an incidence of cases in excess of the expected for the time, the place or the season. Such abnormal incidence occurs from time to time and is usually related to a change in the balance of environmental factors favouring the transmission of the causative disease agent concerned.

*Unusual Outbreak of Disease*
An unusual outbreak of disease may be defined as an outbreak that is unexpected within the prevailing context of environmental parameters. It may, therefore, be unexpected for one or more of the following reasons:

The disease is not endemic within the affected region and locally acquired cases have not be recorded previously.

The disease, although prevalent in the affected region, becomes epidemic outside it's normal season.

The reservoir host and/or insect vector of the disease do not occur in or were eradicated from the affected region.

*M. Dando et al. (eds.),*
*Scientific and Technical Means of Distinguishing Between Natural and Other Outbreaks of Disease, 87–92.*
© 2001 *Kluwer Academic Publishers.*

The disease appears to be transmitted by an uncommon or unusual route, e.g. airborne anthrax.

Outbreak of the disease in a population with a high level of immunity due to vaccination. This may suggest that the cause is a modified agent against which routine vaccination may not be effective. Such modification may be due to deliberate genetic manipulation of the disease agent.

The disease is caused by an agent with an unusually broad antibiotic resistance pattern.

Other indications of the disease being caused by an agent which have undergone genetic modification such as increased virulence and abnormally reduced incubation period.

Outbreak of disease in an unexpected population subset. For example occurance of Rift Valley fever mainly in persons who have no exposure to livestock.

*Unnatural Outbreaks of Disease*
An unnatural outbreak of disease may display the same features and characteristics as an unusual outbreak, but it is from unnatural origin.

## 2. Investigation of Unusual/Unnatural Outbreaks

These investigations could be conducted under difficult circumstances such as time constraints due to urgency to find the source if the outbreak is ongoing or artificial time limits due to public or other pressures. Small numbers of cases to study or difficulty in obtaining clinical and environmental samples if the investigation takes place after the outbreak has been terminated are also complicating factors.

The outcome of an investigation would very much depend on the personnel involved and the techniques they use during the investigation.

### 2.1 INVESTIGATIVE EPIDEMIOLOGY

The techniques used in such an investigation could all be included in the term investigative epidemiology. This would consist of techniques such as case definition, collection and evaluation of background data, clinical examination of cases including laboratory investigation of clinical samples and environmental samples, interviewing of cases as well as their families and when necessary the clinical examination of animals and clinical samples from animals where zoonoses are involved.

### 2.2 DATA COLLECTION CASE DEFINITION

A clinical definition of the disease under investigation should be drawn up to assist identification of true cases and which will exclude individuals suffering from other diseases. The definition should therefore incorporate both inclusive and exclusive criteria. Questionnaires facilitate rapid, standardised data collection and enable the use of non-professional personnel. Questionnaires should make provision for both clinical and epidemiological data.

## 2.3 IDENTIFICATION OF THE CAUSATIVE AGENT

In the investigation of most disease outbreaks, agent identification is usually based on clinical examination and other investigations of the index case/s and utilises information obtained on signs and symptoms of their illness, epidemiological information concerning suspected involvement or otherwise of reservoir hosts, disease vectors, occupational exposure, etc. Routine laboratory tests are used to confirm the suspected diagnosis.

More elaborate laboratory analyses, requiring specialised facilities and/or special centres, may be necessary when investigating an unusual disease outbreak. In the case of bacterial infections, antibiotic sensitivity patterns should always be determined. It may also be necessary to carry out special investigations (employing e.g. various electrophoretic techniques, polymerase chain reaction, DNA sequencing and others) aimed at precise molecular characterisation of the suspected agent.

Genetic analysis of the putative agent, samples of which have been obtained at different times during the outbreak and from widely separated areas, may give an indication as to the source and spread of the outbreak. When unusual reservoir hosts or insect vectors are implicated, samples of these also need to be investigated for the presence of the suspected causative agent.

## 2.4 UTILIZING BACKGROUND INFORMATION AND DATA

To establish whether and outbreak is occurring or has occurred, it is necessary to utilise routine demographic and surveillance data. This can be done by reviewing of hospital, laboratory and other public health records. If outbreak of a "new" disease is investigated, it would be necessary to determine whether or not cases of this disease did occur in the past but went unnoticed or were not reported.

This data can then be utilized to reconstruct previous occurrences of the disease with which the present occurrence can be compared.

## 2.5 IDENTIFICATION OF GEOGRAPHIC CLUSTERING OF CASES

In the investigation of unusual outbreaks of disease it is especially important to plot all cases on a map to identify geographic clustering of cases. Since unusual outbreaks may result from hospital, laboratory or production facility accidents, the location of health care centres and microbiological laboratories and facilities should also be shown.

## 2.6 EPIDEMIC CURVES

Epidemic curves constructed by plotting dates of onset of a single defined clinical feature against the number of cases, are useful to identify mode/s of spread, incubation periods, temporal clustering of cases and other features. The shape of these curves can also be useful to indicate whether the outbreak has a point-source, whether there is ongoing transmission or a combination of the two.

## 2.7 IDENTIFICATION OF UNUSUAL FEATURES

Once the causative agent is known and the necessary background information and data have been obtained, any unusual features of the outbreak should be identified. These would include the nature of the target population and the identity of any animal and/or insect vector species. Where applicable, any other mechanism of transmission or delivery which may be specific to the outbreak in question, should also be identified. These mechanisms may include spread from one individual to another or inter-species spread (e.g. animal-to-human) or dissemination from laboratory/hospital equipment or other devices. Any such installations or devices, if believed to play a role, should also be examined microbiologically.

## 2.8 EXTENT AND SEVERITY OF THE OUTBREAK

The extent and the severity of the outbreak are assessed by calculation of various rates such as attack rates and case fatality rates. By means of a line list, common factors shared by those who are ill are identified. This data is compared with that obtained on healthy controls to calculate attack rates.

## 2.9 HYPOTHESES

Hypotheses regarding the likely cause-effect relationship are drawn up in order to formulate appropriate containment and preventative measures, including continued routine or revised surveillance. Laboratory assistance is of importance at this stage in the confirmation of such hypotheses. These hypotheses then have to be tested by means of various analytical studies, the end result of which could be a conclusion regarding the source of the outbreak and/or recommendations on treatment and measures to prevent further spread or future prevention.

## 3. Composition of the Investigating Team

### 3.1 CORE PERSONNEL

The investigating team should include professional core personnel comprising e.g. appropriate clinicians, epidemiologists and pathologists. The team members must be thoroughly familiar with the normal clinical presentation, epidemiology and pathology of infectious disease and with the variations which naturally occur in accordance with the geographic foci in which they are normally found. Deviations from the norm will thus be readily recognised.

## 3.2 AD HOC TEAM MEMBERS

In accordance with the demands of each specific circumstance, expertise may also be required in other fields such as biosafety, zoology (usually mammology and entomology), botany, clinical and molecular microbiology, toxicology, biochemistry, civil engineering (in some water borne disease outbreaks) and statistics.

## 3.3 LABORATORY SUPPORT

Sophisticated laboratory support capable of conducting all the necessary laboratory investigations is essential especially when proof is required.

## 3.4 SUPPORT SERVICES

In certain cases the availability of persons well versed in logistics, communications and other auxiliary services would be an advantage.


## 4. Differentiation Between Natural and Unnatural Outbreaks

The differentiation between natural and other disease outbreaks may range from fairly simple in cases where biological or toxin weapons have been delivered in munitions during armed conflict, to virtually impossible when an epidemic has been started in a covert fashion with an endemic occurring agent depending on natural spread of the disease.

The investigation approach and techniques would be similar for all outbreaks, whether occurring naturally or unnaturally. In the end the interpretation of investigation results by experts would be the only method to determine the difference. Although there are factors such as the strain of the infectious agent which may differ from the expected and indications that the origin of the disease may be unnatural, a decision would require thorough evaluation of all information. In the absence of "a smoking gun" it would be virtually impossible to provide proof that an outbreak was unnatural in origin.

## References

BWC/AS HOC GROUP/WP.62, 16 July 1996 *Unusual Outbreaks of Disease and their Investigation.*

BWC/AD HOC GROUP/WP.11, 29 November 1995 *Use of Investigative Epidemiology as a Tool in the Investigation of Unusual Outbreaks of Disease and Alleged Use of Biological Weapons.*

Reingold Arthur L. Outbreak Investigations – A Perspective. *EID* 14 (1).

BWC/AD HOC GROUP/WP.73, 17 July 1996 *The Role of Epidemiology in Unusual/Suspicious Outbreaks of Disease*.

Noah Donald L, Sobel Annette L, Ostroff Stephen M, Kildew John A., *Biological Warfare Training : Infectious Disease Outbreak Differentiation Criteria*. undated.

# NATURAL AND OTHER BIOLOGICAL RISKS FROM A MEDICAL SERVICE PERSPECTIVE

T. SOHNS, AND E. J. FINKE
*German Armed Forces Medical Academy*
*Neuherbergstr. 11, D – 80937 Munich*

## 1. New Challenges for the Medical Services

In the days of the East-West confrontation, the possible use of nuclear and chemical weapons in a war could have caused losses that threatened life itself and the disastrous destruction of infrastructure among all the warring parties. This is why many people at that time questioned the benefit of medical NBC defense activities. The situation is quite the opposite today, where the chief risks emanating from NBC weapons are considered to lie in the exposure of a force contingent "out of area". Hence, the benefit of medical NBC defense activities is now in an utterly different light, for national resources would be available for saving the lives of casualties.

The ability to use armed forces in international crisis management missions is highly dependent upon the relationship that exists between risks to health and the capability to maintain and restore health. Troops dispatched on crisis management missions outside their home countries, where peace still prevails, are entitled to a medical care at their mission locations which is equivalent in standard to the care they would receive in their home countries. This principle also applies to operations in an NBC environment.

## 2. Natural Biological Risks to be Considered

In many areas of the world including potential theatres of operations, there may be sources of communicable diseases with whose micro-organisms the immune systems of travellers (business), tourists and soldiers have not yet come into contact. This means that the indigenous population may be largely immune, while travellers, tourists and soldiers are unprotected. Against the background of natural disasters such as earthquakes and floods, or of civil wars such as the situation in the former Yugoslavia, medical services must also bear in mind the possibility of having to work in disaster areas where epidemics are a risk. Epidemiological data bases can be highly instrumental in coping with these risks.

One aspect of natural biological risks which cannot be covered by epidemiological data bases but which is very significant for considerations about biological weapons is "emerging and re-emerging infectious diseases." In the last two decades, some 30 previously unknown infectious diseases have emerged. They include the HI-virus, with which millions of people have become infected. Other familiar examples are Ebola and Marburg haemorrhagic fever. At the same time, known infectious diseases such as

93

*M. Dando et al. (eds.),*
*Scientific and Technical Means of Distinguishing Between Natural and Other Outbreaks of Disease*, 93–100.
© 2001 *Kluwer Academic Publishers.*

tuberculosis and diphtheria, which appeared to have been overcome, are on the advance again. This problem is rendered more complicated by the rising frequency of resistance to antibiotics. A key factor governing this development is the fact that there is a worldwide reduction in public health activities, notably in monitoring, and there is less and less laboratory capacity available for use in quickly spotting problems.

The potential of epidemics to *spread* is also vastly increasing due to major changes in contemporary living. The growing number of overcrowded cities with poor water and sanitation offer fertile media for propagating disease. The war-induced migration of refugees and their accommodation in camps under austere conditions is another problem to be taken into consideration. A particular contemporary factor in the spread of disease arises from the dramatic increase in international travel, which allows an individual infected in one country to quickly carry a disease to other countries before actually falling ill.

## 3. Other Biological Risks

Something that is far more dangerous and far more unpredictable than endemic diseases in potential theatres are the risks posed by the proliferation of biological weapons.[1] Despite the large-scale efforts being made throughout the world to promote disarmament and arms control, both governments and civil war parties, as well as terrorists and other criminal forces may acquire biological weapons or gain access to them in the foreseeable future.

Continuous improvements in biotechnology have made it possible to produce biological agents in smaller facilities with dual use technology. The risk of secret production and proliferation has increased accordingly.

Apart from the risk of biological weapons being employed there is also a risk that accidents in biological research and development facilities, in particular in BW production plants, may lead to the release of extremely pathogenic material.

## 3.1 BIOLOGICAL WEAPONS ARE DIFFERENT

A special feature of biological weapons is the width of the potential attack spectrum. It ranges from action by an individual to the possibility of a strategic attack. A biological attack can be carried out clandestinely or in the open, irrespective of its size. This is not possible with any other kind of weapon. It is also possible to combine biological agents with radiological and chemical weapons. UNSCOM investigated traces that apparently lead to Iraqi work on weapons filled with a mix of biological and chemical agents. Medical services would be confronted with patients displaying unknown syndromes. At the same time, medical services would be required to make major contributions to identifying the cause.

Another special feature is the fact that some biological weapons can cause the outbreak of epidemics. This feature is indeed unique. No other ammunition reproduces after it has been employed. Containment of an epidemic will present a major problem to medical services and will put much pressure on military and political decision makers. One particular challenge for medical services posed by biological weapons is their potential for mimicry. This is the ability of biological agents to mimic natural diseases. This property can be put to highly perfidious use when biological agents are released clandestinely.

Firstly, it may be extremely difficult to distinguish the effects of biological weapons from quite natural causes, notably when micro-organisms are selected that also occur naturally in the theatre. The target party would have to prove to the international community that the cause of the outbreak of an epidemic or a case of mass intoxication was "man-made." Secondly, there is no way of ruling out the possibility of genetically modified micro-organisms being used for a biological weapon. If that were the case, verification authorities would face the problem of differentiating a "man-made" cause from a natural, so-called "emerging" infectious disease.

## 4. Diagnostic Problems

In order to demonstrate what it may mean, if an *emerging and re-emerging infectious disease* or just a *normal epidemic* has to be differentiated from a *man-made outbreak*, three recent events will serve as examples:

### 4.1 THE SVERDLOVSK ANTHRAX EPIDEMIC

In April and May 1979, an outbreak of anthrax occurred in what was then known as Sverdlovsk (now Ekaterinburg), a city east of the Urals, in which 96 cases of sickness and 64 deaths were reported.

Official sources claimed that the outbreak was caused by gastrointestinal anthrax contracted by the consumption of contaminated meat. The USA and other western countries, however, had their doubts about the Soviet version and, suspecting a possible violation of the BTWC,[2] made an effort to analyse the occurrence. In discussions with foreign analysts, Soviet physicians who worked in the epidemic focus continued to support the official version. Only in 1991 was an official investigation of the 1979 epidemic ordered by President Yeltsin. In his decree of 1992, he stated that the outbreak had been the result of activities taking place in military microbiological facilities in Sverdlovsk. The epidemiological, clinical and aerobiological analysis of available data conducted since this time and the patho-anatomical and recent molecular biological examinations of organs, in particular pulmonary tissue samples from corpses, now make it appear extremely plausible that the inhalation of anthrax spores was the cause of the epidemic. Until now, there have been different interpretations of the cause of the anthrax spores release. Theories include an accident in the ventilation system as well as the explosion of a piece of cassette ammunition in Unit 19. We may safely assume, however, that an accident in Unit 19 released an anthrax spores aerosol which could have spread some 50 - 75 km over the area of the city and the surrounding villages. This assessment is based primarily on studies conducted by Meselson and Abramova, on interviews with officials of the civilian and military administration of Sverdlovsk, and on allegations forwarded by Kanatjan Alibekov, a former deputy director of the Biopreparat complex.

## 4.2 THE PLAGUE EPIDEMIC IN SURAT

The second example is the plague epidemic which occurred in the Indian state of Surat. The course of the outbreak was typical of a BW attack with subsequent secondary waves of epidemics.

On September 19, 1994, a pneumonic plague epidemic broke out among primarily young male migrant workers in Surat during the traditional festival in honour of the rat king. These men had recently arrived from an area in which shortly before the rat and bubonic plague had broken out after a respite of ten years. In total, more than 970 people had fallen ill in Surat by November 1994, with 450 of these most likely having contracted the plague. 52 of the patients died, and in some 25 cases we are now certain, thanks to microbiological analyses, that the cause of death was pneumonic plague.

Shortly after the outbreak, rumours circulated in the Indian press that this could have been a terrorist attack carried out by Kashmir separatists. They were said to have obtained a genetically manipulated plague strain from a research institute in Alma Ata, the capital of Kirghizia, and to have sprayed it on the festival. The director of this institute made an official statement in which he vehemently rejected such allegations.

What complicated the investigation of this incident was the panic which was publicised by the media - ours as well - and which spread among the frightened inhabitants and members of the medical community, some of whom also fled the city. This was the reason for the delay in the epidemiological and microbiological investigations; the samples were either too small or were taken only after the patients had received initial treatment with antibiotics. In many cases, the tentative diagnosis of infection with *Yersinia pestis*, the plague pathogen, could only be substantiated by serologic tests carried out at a later date. The early microbiological findings of local laboratories, which for the most part used classical bacteriological procedures, at first pointed towards melioidosis. In actual fact, this disease is common in India and may have a course similar to that of pneumonic plague.

In patients who have inhaled *Yersinia pestis* aerosols, we can generally expect to find a pronounced increase in germs in the body along with sepsis. Appropriate diagnostic facilities were, however, unavailable in Surat at the beginning of the epidemic. It was not before the close of 1996 that a group of experts from WHO along with specialists of the CDC in Atlanta, the Pasteur Institute in Paris and the Gamaleia Institute in Moscow together with their Indian colleagues from New Delhi succeeded in confirming the original tentative diagnosis of pneumonic plague. This was done primarily with the help of molecular biological techniques such as the polymerase chain reaction. In the case of PCR the DNA of specific plague virulence genes can be extracted from the lungs of a number of plague corpses, multiplied up to a million times the initial quantity with the help of PCR, and then identified by gel electrophoresis analysis.

However, let us return now to the suspicions that the plague epidemic in Surat was caused by the release of a biological warfare agent. Even the specialised tests mentioned, which were used by the WHO experts, were unable to verify or rule out this suspicion with any degree of certainty. Scientists thus attempted to conduct a differential diagnosis using the few saved plague isolates based on the ribonucleic acid specific to each strain. As a result, they were able to confirm that only ribotypes of *Yersinia pestis* were involved which are characteristic of west India.

This brings us to a significant problem of diagnosing biological warfare injuries: It is not unusual to have virtually no chance of cultivating pathogens from victims if, as is absolutely essential in the case of pneumonic plague or pulmonary anthrax, high doses of antibiotics have been administered at the first sign of these diseases. Just imagine the significance a similar event could assume at an international trouble-spot. The following example may give you an idea what this could mean.

4.3. THE TULAREMIA OUTBREAK IN NORTHERN BOSNIA

In early 1995, the parties to the war in northern Bosnia accused each other of using biological weapons to produce outbreaks of tularemia. These allegations must be considered now when analysing the general risks for the UN troops stationed in the former Yugoslavia. Whether they are at risk from biological exposure cannot be answered with any certainty. We must keep in mind the fact that tularemia pathogens are suitable for use in biological weapons and have been weaponised. On the other hand, these allegations have never been verified and tularemia is also a naturally occurring disease in Bosnia.

Further investigations are necessary. The reservoirs of tularemia in Bosnia's animal world should be examined in order to distinguish between two different strains: The highly virulent tularemia pathogen type A (*Francisella tularensis* var. *tularensis*) which is endemic in North America and the less dangerous pathogen type B (*Francisella tularensis* var. *palaearctica*) which is endemic in Europe and parts of Asia. Type B tularemia is endemic in Bosnia. Therefore, should evidence be found of Type A, which is not known to be endemic there, the possibility cannot be ruled out that outbreaks of tularemia were brought about by biological weapons. With this in mind it should not be ignored, however, that type A tularemia could also have found its way to Bosnia by other means, e.g. as a result of previous biological research and development activities in the former Eastern bloc.

5. Particular Risks in Crisis Management Missions

When we consider how time-consuming and perhaps extremely difficult the process of identification generally is at the moment, we can clearly see the particular risk posed by the clandestine use of such weapons. This is even more significant for international crisis management missions, which are normally characterised by the absence of large-scale fighting. As it is not generally possible to use conventional weapons in obscurity, parties in civil wars, or terrorists even, may find biological (and chemical) weapons highly attractive, on account of their ability to be used clandestinely. This also renders the principle of deterrence largely obsolete. They can be used inside and outside the crisis area. Armed forces personnel as well as civilians can be exposed to biological agents, irrespective of the selected target. Regardless of the number of casualties produced by a biological attack, it would place enormous pressure on the governments of countries providing armed forces for the international crisis management mission.

## 6. The Gaps

Account must also be taken of the fact that broad technological and medical gaps still remain with regard to biological weapons. For example, there are currently no reliable early-warning systems in operation that enable armed forces or the civil population to be warned, if necessary at night, when they are asleep, that a biological aerosol cloud is drawing close. The protection of troops which can generally be provided by means of immunisation is also limited for medical and other (political, legal, emotional) reasons. The absence of an effective therapy constitutes another major medical gap. Closing the technological gaps that exist, though primarily the medical ones, is a difficult job as it is; the large number and large variety of potential micro-organisms and toxins, however, make it even more so.

## 7. Conclusions

### 7.1 THE PROTECTIVE TRIAD: POLITICAL, NBC DEFENSIVE AND MEDICAL COUNTERMEASURES

No strategy can at present guarantee full protection against risks from biological weapons. There is no magic pill, and there is no impregnable shield. The best possible defense is a joint approach in which political, NBC defensive and medical measures mutually complement and enhance one another:

a) To the greatest extent possible, the risk of a biological attack should be ruled out by political measures including disarmament and arms control. These measures are laid down in the BTWC and follow-on agreements.

b) Political measures, however, do not offer complete protection. Therefore, the military and civilian technological activities (dual use problem!) of "rogue states" along with the activities of suspicious persons and organisations must continuously be observed, analysed and evaluated in an attempt to recognise biological activities conducted for non-peaceful purposes. This increases the chances of preventing the employment of biological weapons and of developing effective countermeasures.

Should prevention fail, armed forces must be prepared to defend themselves by finding and destroying enemy biological weapons and through the rapid detection of agents, protection and decontamination. *Biological defense capability* will protect personnel and materiel against exposure to biological agents. It will serve to:

- prevent casualties as well as damage to materiel and facilities and reduce the effects of biological weapons;
- maintain or restore the operational capability of units affected by biological weapons.

For medical services, this means that measures must be taken to protect medical personnel, patients and medical facilities against exposure to biological agents. In this specific area medical services have a lot to catch up on. One of the effects of being capable of protecting one's forces against biological weapons is that it renders biological weapon programs less attractive.

c) Since biological defense, too, cannot guarantee complete protection, medical capabilities must be available to:

- maintain and restore the health of personnel exposed to biological agents;
- clarify the causes of puzzling diseases and deaths, e.g. to differentiate natural from other outbreaks;
- advise political and military decision makers.

Medical considerations must include not only the acute, often lethal effects of biological weapons but also, and increasingly, the long-term effects of low-dose exposure to biological agents.

## 7.2 FUTURE CHALLENGES

Armed forces of the future must have the capability to protect themselves against biological exposure and, where precautionary measures fail, they must be able to restore the health of those personnel who have been exposed. State-of-the-art equipment and procedures need to be in place. Armed forces which do not have this capability cannot participate within the Alliance. Nor will they be able to provide effective assistance should their own country find itself under biological threat.

## 7.3 PROTECTION OF THE CIVIL POPULATION

Above and beyond military considerations, it must be remembered that in many countries the civilian sector has seen its civil defense resources substantially reduced since the end of the Cold War. As far as the management of situations involving biological hazards in the civilian sector is concerned, such as the threat or the actual use of biological weapons in terrorist attacks, the armed forces' NBC medical defense expertise may be the only national resource available to decision makers for well-founded judgements.

## 7.4 CONTINUITY AND LONG TERM PLANNING: THE ONLY WAY FORWARD

While it is quite normal for the perception of a particular risk to oscillate, the future availability of medical and other scientific capabilities is not possible without continuity and long-term planning. For day-to-day medical care, this is not a problem since with the exception of a disaster, e.g. an epidemic, the type and frequency of diseases and injuries change only very slowly in peacetime and, what is more, there are thousands of competent people with the necessary knowledge and experience.

In NBC medical defense the situation is quite different. Clinical pictures of relevance to NBC medical defense occur, if at all, only seldom, and then mostly in connection with armed conflicts or terrorist acts. Accordingly, only few countries have even one facility working in this field ("scientific islands"). Such facilities are usually just big enough to be able to fulfil their personnel requirements for their own regular (small group of) experts. But if continuity and long-term planning are disrupted at such nationally or internationally unique establishments in response to diminishing risk perceptions, the result will be irreversible damage.

A nation's NBC medical defense can therefore simply not afford to adapt to changing risk perceptions, because the point of no return is always close. Having once passed this point, capabilities cannot be reactivated in five or ten years, not even with huge amounts of money. For the eventuality that such an adjustment to decreasing risk perception is seriously considered, all decision makers must be warned that it is not possible to turn back down a one-way street.

**Notes**

[1] Biological weapons consist of biological agents and delivery systems. Biological agents are reproductive microorganisms and toxins of biological origin which are produced for non-peaceful purposes and whose effects on physioligical processes can result in death, temporary incapacitation or permanent damage.

[2] Convention on the Prohibition of the Development, Production and Stockpiling of Bacteriological (Biological) and Toxin Weapons and on Destruction, 1972.

# THE WHO ROLE IN SURVEILLANCE AND CONTROL OF EMERGING INFECTIOUS DISEASES

R. D'AMELIO°, O.COSIVI* AND D.L. HEYMANN*

°Ministry of Defence, General Directorate for Military Health, Rome (Italy)
*World Health Organisation, Geneva (Switzerland)

## 1. Introduction

Infectious diseases remain an important cause of suffering and death. They disproportionately affect the poorest populations of developing countries. In 1997, infectious diseases were responsible for 33% of more than 50 million deaths worldwide.[1]

Infectious diseases may readily be transmitted through direct and indirect contact, by improperly processed or stored food and, in the case of zoonoses, by infected animals and animal products. Incidence is affected by the infectivity and virulence of the agent, the type and rate of contact between hosts and it is directly proportional to the number or density of susceptible hosts. Globalisation has made new and re-emerging infections a concern for the entire world[2]. And there is a fear that some infectious diseases could also be intentionally caused[3]. There have been well over 29 outbreaks of emerging or re-emerging diseases reported to the World Health Organisation (WHO) during the past two years and these outbreaks require immediate investigation and containment wherever they occur.

Infectious diseases could lead to international political crisis and severe social and economic disruptions. The equivalent of US$770 million was the estimated loss due to trade embargo on seafood exports caused by the cholera epidemic in Peru in 1991. The same is true for a recent embargo on fresh water fish from East Africa, where Tanzania alone estimated a loss of up to US$32.2 million in 1997. Plague cost India in 1994 up to US$1.7 billion in decreased trade and tourism and the current Bovine Spongiform Encephalopathy (BSE) outbreak has be estimated to have cost the UK economy over US$38 Billion to date.

## 2. Current Status of Preventive and Therapeutic Means

Since 1950 there have been over 30 vaccines licensed to prevent common childhood and adult infections.[4] However, effective vaccines to prevent the major endemic diseases such as adult tuberculosis, malaria, gonorrhoea and Human Immunodeficiency Virus (HIV) are not yet available. The situation concerning the discovery of new antimicrobial agents is more alarming. There has been a steady decrease in the rate of discovery of new antibiotics since the 1960s and the cost of developing new drugs

M. Dando et al. (eds.),
Scientific and Technical Means of Distinguishing Between Natural and Other Outbreaks of Disease, 101–109.
© 2001 Kluwer Academic Publishers.

continues to increase. Even more alarming, antimicrobial resistance has evolved at a rapid pace.[5] *Staphylococcus aureus* resistance to penicillin was first detected in 1946. Today resistance exceeds 80% in some communities and up to 95% in some hospitals. And a similar picture has occurred with first line antimicrobials used to treat other infectious diseases, such as tuberculosis[6,7] and HIV.[8,9] Antimicrobial resistance is mainly a human problem, caused by misuse in and by humans. But it is also a problem in animals. Zoonotic organisms resistant in animals have the potential to transfer to humans.[5,10,11] In the Netherlands, beginning in 1984, there has been a steady increase in resistance of *Salmonella typhimurium* in pigs. A similar trend has occurred in human infections. Though transfer of resistant organisms has not been proven in this instance, the temporal and geographic association demand further study.

Globalisation has justifiably made infectious diseases in one country a concern of the entire world. Today resistant microorganisms are spread worldwide in human vectors. Two multiresistant clones of *Streptococcus pneumoniae* were first identified in Spain, then within a very short period, throughout the world.[5]

## 3. Global Situation and WHO Strategy

Globalisation in health is therefore a great concern for both individuals and developing countries. In industrialised countries it is an issue related to national and international public health security. In developing countries it is an issue of early detection and containment to avoid damage to fragile economies. The common issue to both is strong global and national surveillance and control, as well as an opportunity to move resources for public health from the North to the South. But the fight against infectious diseases requires a global partnership. It can not be won by any one country or multilateral group alone. A global alert requires an ever broadening global response of partnerships, both technical and financial and new partnerships must be developed, using private and other non-governmental sectors The recent response to an extended outbreak of human monkeypox in Democratic Republic of Congo (former Zaire) shows the types of partnership required.[12] The outbreak was first reported to WHO by Médicins sans Frontiéres (MSF) in August 1996 and a WHO-led local team conducted a preliminary investigation in September, providing specimens to the WHO Collaborating Centre on orthopox infections. After the monkeypox virus was identified, an investigation was undertaken in January 1997 with technical partners from the Centers for Disease Control and Prevention, Atlanta, USA (CDC) and the European Programme on Intervention Epidemiology Training (EPIET). The investigation was interrupted in February by civil war and begun again in September with a team broadened to include the Public Health Laboratory Services of the United Kingdom (PHLS). Intensified post-epidemic surveillance began in January of 1998 with financial support from the National Institute of Health of the USA, the European Union and WHO, and with continuing laboratory support from CDC and PHLS. Once results from this uncharacteristically large outbreak of human monkeypox have been analysed, a WHO consensus meeting will be held, obtaining guidance from the world's experts on the public health implications of this outbreak.

WHO can catalyse such global partnerships and can ensure that the cost of international response does not fall on any one country or technical partner. At WHO, a global framework in which partners can work together in the fight against infectious diseases has been set up. The framework contains 4 major areas:

1) global surveillance, monitoring and alert;
2) global preparedness and control;
3) global information access and exchange;
4) national surveillance and control.

## 3.1 GLOBAL SURVEILLANCE, MONITORING AND ALERT

Global surveillance, monitoring and alert has the objective of strengthening WHO information networks on infectious and zoonotic diseases to ensure early detection of global threats to public health. In addition to linking with other established networks, WHO's contribution in this area is a strengthening on its own Collaborating Centre networks in viral, bacteria and zoonotic diseases.

The network for arbovirus and haemorrhagic fevers is one of such networks. It is geographically complete. However, work remains to be done: electronic links must be assured between all laboratories and with WHO so that when there is a disease, or even a simple need for reagents or training, a rapid response can be provided. Another such network is the WHO influenza network, which links national networks, individual national influenza laboratories, WHO Collaborating Centres in influenza and WHO. Constant isolation and sequencing of influenza viruses by this network makes it possible twice each year to recommend the constitution of influenza vaccine for the northern and then the southern hemispheres. It was in one of these Collaborating Laboratories that the H5N1 human strain of avian influenza isolated in Hong Kong was first identified in late 1997, and with the cooperation of other WHO Collaborating Laboratories, a major epidemic response was initiated.[13]

Another very important global monitoring and alert system is The International Health Regulations, the only international public health legislation requiring reporting of infectious diseases: plague, yellow fever and cholera. They also set out standards and norms to prevent the spread of infectious diseases at ports of entry. However, the disease coverage is narrow and the names of these diseases inevitably cause stigmatisation, which may lead to the imposition of very costly international trade sanctions and embargoes for the affected countries. Very often, countries are reluctant to report these diseases because of the possible socio-economic consequences of international sanctions imposed on fragile national economies. Revision of The Regulations has begun to provide broader disease coverage.[14] Initial reporting will become less stigmatising by reporting outbreaks/epidemics of 5 different identified syndromes with potential international implications. The syndromes under field-testing are: acute neurological, haemorrhagic, gastrointestinal, pulmonary and jaundice associated syndromes. The revision is also exploring ways to improve reporting and incorporate a response mechanism. After field testing, The Regulations will become a functional alert and response systems through electronic links to focal points in all Member States. Links with the World Trade Organisation (WTO) will minimise the impact of disease reporting on economies.

Informal information from various unofficial sources is routinely collected by WHO through networks such as The Program for Monitoring Emerging Diseases (ProMED),[15] media, professional networks and specialised early warning systems such as the Global Public Health Information Network (GPHIN).[16] Information is then processed through the WHO outbreak verification system which involves contacting the WHO regional Offices, WHO field offices and, if needed, other partners present in the field (e.g. Non-Governmental Organisations), requesting them to provide further information on the event of interest, as well as offering technical support for disease containment. All verified outbreaks are then reported back through the weekly "outbreak verification list" to all information providers. Once an outbreak has been officially confirmed by the interested Member State, the information on this event is then provided through the world wide web or published in the Weekly Epidemiological Record. In 1997 this system investigated 128 reported events. Over 97% of these events were verified as outbreaks and in 65% laboratory diagnosis was confirmed.

In addition to these well established surveillance tools, WHO plans to involve health military facilities in the public health surveillance activities. The justifications for liasing with military health system are:

1) the military is a population at special risk for infectious diseases;
2) military laboratories, in some developed countries, have better capabilities than public health laboratories.

The first activity of this project included a survey among all WHO member States to identify countries interested in collaborating through their military health laboratory capable of diagnosing common infectious and/or notifying infectious diseases through the national reporting system. This was followed by a second survey, where diagnostic and reporting practices were assessed.[17] The third stage will include joint training workshops of public health and military health personnel of developing countries and the establishment of electronic links for exchange of information among laboratories.

Up to now, out of 107 countries to which an adhesion to the project has been requested, 76 have replied, involving 25/34 (73%) from Africa, 14/28 (50%) from Asia, 9/17 (53%) from the Americas, 26/26 (100%) from Europe, Australia and New Zealand. A military laboratory able to diagnose endemic infectious diseases and to recognise the presence of unusual ones is present in 19/25 (76%) African countries, in 17/26 (68%) European countries, in 5/9 (55%) American countries, in 12/14 (86%) Asian countries and it is absent in Oceania; the total is 53/76 (70%). A military notifications system for infectious diseases is present in 19/25 (76%) African countries, in 24/26 (92%) European countries, in 7/9 (78%) American countries, in 11/14 (79%) Asian countries and in 1/2 Oceanian countries; the grand total is 62/76 (82%).

A second series of questionnaires was sent to the 76 countries which first replied, asking for more detailed information on the diagnostic capabilities of the laboratories, the characteristics of the notification system, the mandatory diagnostic schedule for infectious diseases on recruitment, if present, and the actual vaccinations schedule.

Out of 76 countries contacted, 52 replied: 15 from Africa, 5 from the Americas, 7 from Asia, 23 from Europe and 2 from Oceania. Among these 52, 39 (75%) have a military laboratory to diagnose infectious diseases, 23 (46%) of whom declare to be able to undertake at least 4 of the following activities: Bacteriology, Virology, Parasitology, Immunology and Molecular Biology. Thirty-five (67%) out of 52 have expressed their interest to participate in WHO antibiotic resistance monitoring and containment programme.

Twenty-seven (52%) of the countries are equipped with a computerised network for surveillance and 16 countries (31%) report not having a system to avoid duplicate notification of the same disease with the national public health service. Finally, 4 countries do not notify their national public health services about infectious diseases occurring in the military population.

Forty-three (83%) countries perform mandatory screening on recruitment for tuberculosis and/or syphilis, 27 (52%) for HIV infection, while some screen for other viral diseases, such as hepatitis A virus (HAV), hepatitis B virus (HBV) and/or hepatitis C virus (HCV) (one African country requires screening for HAV and HBV, but not for HIV). Twenty one (40%) perform a mandatory screening on recruitment for intestinal, urinary and/or blood-borne parasitic diseases.

Five of the 52 countries have no mandatory general immunisation schedule. Of the remaining 47 (90%), 45 (87%) countries require immunisation against tetanus, toxoid, 30 against diphtheria toxoid, 23 against typhoid fever, 16 require immunisation with the Bacillus Calmette Guerin (BCG), 16 with polio vaccine, 11 with meningococcal meningitis vaccine and 10 with trivalent measles, mumps and rubella vaccines. Two countries still report vaccinia vaccinations as compulsory for military recruits.

WHO is also planning to include some of the personnel of the military health laboratories of developing countries in training courses on bacteriology, with the aim to bringing them into the network of antibiotic resistance monitoring. This will be the first step to allow the laboratories to actually work together. Once organised, the military network for surveillance of infectious diseases and antimicrobial resistance will be useful for detecting and monitoring both naturally occurring or deliberately caused outbreaks of infectious diseases.

## 3.2 GLOBAL PREPAREDNESS AND CONTROL

This area of WHO actively sets international standards and norms; once international norms have been derived, they are widely distributed. Recently, WHO recommended surveillance standards have been published and distributed as hard copy as well as made available through the world wide web.[18] They provide case definitions for 56 common infectious diseases and syndromes. Three different case definitions are given for 36 diseases based on the level of diagnostic and laboratory support available. Such standards make possible international collaborative activities on global surveillance.

International consensus is regularly obtained by WHO from the world's experts on issues of international public health importance. In the case of the recent emergence of the BSE and the new variant of Creutzfeldt-Jakob disease (nvCJD), WHO has provided a neutral forum in which to address issues for which scientific information has of necessity been slow to obtain.[19-23] This neutral forum has permitted periodic review of recommendations in light of new scientific information as it has become available.

Another WHO initiative in this area of activity is the update of the 1970 WHO publication *Health Aspects of Chemical and Biological Weapons*.[24] WHO in close collaboration with a selected and geographically well balanced group of leading scientists is revising this publication, that should be available in early 1999, nearly 30 years after the first edition. Once published, this book will represent a useful tool for decision makers, public health authorities and their specialist advisers in order to address the public health preparedness and response activities in case of emergencies caused by the deliberate use of chemical or biological agents.

## 3.3 GLOBAL INFORMATION ACCESS AND EXCHANGE

This activity area of the WHO framework ensures that validated health information is available 24 hours a day to the interested people. Examples are represented by prototype world wide web pages for Rabies and Influenza, Rabnet[25] and Flunet.[26] It can be anticipated that within the next 4 to 5 years these prototype systems, into which laboratories and ministries of health enter into their own quality assured data, will cover all infectious diseases of global importance.

## 3.4 NATIONAL SURVEILLANCE AND CONTROL

This final activity area in the WHO framework is the most crucial, implemented through the WHO regional offices, WHO country offices, and ah-hoc programmes and activities, it ensures integrates and intersectoral disease surveillance, prevention and control. Strong national surveillance and control will eventually provide a stronger base for detection and containment of endemic and epidemic infectious diseases.

In this connection, the Mediterranean Zoonoses Control Programme (MZCP) is one example in which WHO facilitates close international and intersectoral collaboration among national authorities of the health and agriculture sectors of countries with similar socio-sanitary models.[27] The MZCP, with the collaboration of regional partner institutions, focuses its work on strengthening surveillance and control on priority zoonotic diseases. In 1978 the countries of the Mediterranean and Middle East areas realised that zoonoses and zoonotic foodborne diseases, such as brucellosis, echinococcosis, leishmaniasis, rabies and zoonotic salmonellosis, could not be efficiently controlled or eliminated if prevention, surveillance and control activities were carried out in isolation by individual countries. Timely exchange between countries of reliable information on disease occurrence, sustained intercountry technical co-operation, harmonisation of surveillance and control strategies and legislation and strong intersectoral collaboration between public health and animal health sectors, are essential for the success of national programmes for zoonoses prevention, surveillance and control.

Strengthening integrated and intersectoral surveillance and control activities through an ad hoc national programme is another important activity. WHO headquarters jointly with the WHO regional office for the Eastern Mediterranean (EMRO) and in collaboration with the United Nations Development Programme (UNDP) is assisting the Palestinian authority to implement a programme for the surveillance and control of human and animal brucellosis in the West Bank and the Gaza Strip.

## 4. Conclusions

Infectious diseases still are a major public health problem in both developing and industrialised nations. The tools to diagnose, prevent and control infectious diseases exist. There is no excuse to not place health at the centre of economic development and to decrease mortality and morbidity from infectious diseases to a minimum.

We must keep in the forefront a vision for the 21st century of a world on the alert and able to contain infectious diseases through a strong base of national disease surveillance and control which feeds into global networks to monitor disease – global networks which ensure timely electronic exchange of information and effective response in countries which have not yet developed the capacity to respond to their own.

## Notes

[1] *The World Health Report 1998. Life in the 21st century – A vision for all*. World Health Organisation, Geneva 1998.
[2] Heymann DL: Emerging and other infectious diseases: epidemiology and control. *World Health Organisation Statistics Quarterly*, 1997: **50** (3-4); 158-60.
[3] Cole LA: The spectre of biological weapons. *Scientific American* 1996; **275**:60-65.
[4] Mandell: *Principle and practice of infectious diseases*. NY Churchill Livingstone, 1995.
[5] Levy SB: The Challenge of antibiotics resistance. *Scientific American* 1998; **278**: 46-55.
[6] Pablos-Méndez A, Raviglione M, Laszlo A, et al: Global Surveillance for anti-tuberculosis drug resistance. 1994-7. *N Engl J Med* 1998; **338**: 1641-9.
[7] Snider DE jr, Castro KG: The global threat of drug-resistant tuberculosis. *N Engl J Med* 1998; **338**: 1689-90.

8   Hecht FM, Grant RM, Petropulos CJ, et al: Sexual transmission of an HIV-1 variant resistant to multiple reverse-transcriptase and protease inhibitors. *N Engl J Med* 1998; **339**: 307-11.

9   Cohen OJ, Fauci AS: Transmission of multidrug-resistant human immunodeficiency virus. The wake up cal. *N Engl J Med* 1998; **339**:341-3.

10  Levy SB: Multidrug resistance – A sign of the times. *N Engl J Med* 1998; **338**: 1376-8.

11  *The Medical Impact of the use of Antimicrobials in Food Animals.* Report of a WHO Meeting, Berlin, Germany. 13-17 October 1997. WHO/EMC/ZOO/97.4.

12  Human Monkeypox in Kasai Oriental, Democratic Republic of the Congo (former Zaire): Preliminary report of October 1997 investigation. *Weekly Epidemiological Record* 1997; **72**: 369-372.

13  *International Effort to Combat New Influenza Strain Stepped Up.* World Health Organization. Geneva. Press Release WHO/92, December 1997.

14  *The International Response to Epidemics and Application of the International Health Regulations.* Report of a WHO Informal Consultation, Geneva, Switzerland 11-14 December 1995. World Health Organisation, Geneva. WHO/EMC/IHR/96.1.

15  http://www.healthnet.org/progammes/promed.html.

16  http://gphin.exocom.com.

17  *WHO recommended surveillance standards.* World health organisation, Geneva, 1997. WHO/EMC/DIS/97.1 (also available in http://www.who.ch/emcsurveill/survdoc.html).

18  D'Amelio R, Heymann DL: Can the military contribute to global surveillance and control of infectious diseases? *Emerging Infectious Diseases* (in press).

19  *Report of a WHO Consultation on Public Health issues related to Animal and Human Spongiform Encephalopathies.* Geneva, 12-14 November 1991. WHO/CDS/VPH/92.104.

20  *Report of a WHO Consultation on Public Health issues related to Human and Animal Transmissible Spongiform Encephalopathies.* Geneva, 17-19 May 1995. WHO/CDS/VPH/95.145.

21  *Report of a WHO Consultation on Public Health issues related to Human and Animal Transmissible Spongiform Encephalopathies.* Geneva, 2-3 April 1996. WHO/EMC/DIS/96.147.

22  *Report of a WHO Consultation on Clinical and Neuropathological Characteristics of the New Variant TSE.* Geneva 14-16 May 1996. WHO/EMC/ZOO/96.1.

23  *Report of a WHO Consultation on Medicinal and other Products in Relation to Human and Animal TSE.* Geneva 24-26 March 1997. WHO/EMC/ZOO/97.3.

24  *Health Aspects of Chemical and Biological Weapons.* World Health Organisation. Geneva, 1970.

25  http://oms.b3e.jussieu.fr/rabnet/.

26  http://oms.b3e.jussieu.fr/rabnet/.

27   *The Mediterranean Zoonoses Control Programme.* Fact Sheet No 185, November
1997. World Health Organisation, Geneva.

# REPORTING OF OUTBREAKS OF DISEASE UNDER BTWC CONFIDENCE-BUILDING MEASURES

ERHARD GEISSLER* AND JOHN P. WOODALL**

* Max-Delbrück Center for Molecular Medicine, Berlin-Buch, Germany,
** Department of Medical Biochemistry, Federal University of Rio de Janeiro, Brazil

## 1. Introduction

The Second Review Conference of the States Parties to the Biological and Toxin Weapons Convention (BTWC) in 1986 realized that the BTWC needed to be strengthened. The conference adopted a set of confidence-building measures (CBMs) designed to provide greater transparency with respect to activities directly related to the BTWC[1].

One reason for the adoption of CBMs was the then increasing suspicion that an outbreak of anthrax in the city of Sverdlovsk was not due to contaminated meat as maintained by the Soviet government, but to an accident in a BW facility.[2,3] Not least for that reason Australia and other Western states proposed that "the Conference requests States Parties to provide without delay detailed information to other States Parties of unusual abnormal large-scale outbreaks of infectious diseases and similar occurrences caused by toxins".[4] The Second Review Conference followed that proposal and decided that the States Parties "are to implement", *inter alia*, an "exchange of information on all outbreaks of infectious diseases and similar occurrences caused by toxins that seem to deviate from the normal pattern as regards type, development, place, or time of occurrence. If possible, the information provided would include, as soon as it is available, data on the type of disease, approximate area affected, and number of cases".[1]

## 2. Modalities for the exchange of information and data

In 1987 the modalities for the CBMs were elaborated by an *Ad Hoc* Meeting of experts convened by the Second Review Conference.[5] The *Ad Hoc* Meeting agreed, *inter alia*, on the modalities for reports on outbreaks and requested States Parties both to provide background information on diseases caused by organisms which meet the criteria for risk groups III and IV as defined by the 1983 WHO Laboratory Biosafety Manual as well as reports on outbreaks that deviate from the normal pattern.

When the CBMs were agreed it was generally understood that only reports on outbreaks of human diseases had been considered, although the Final Declaration of the Second Review Conference stated "that the States Parties are to implement... Exchange of

111

M. Dando et al. (eds.),
*Scientific and Technical Means of Distinguishing Between Natural and Other Outbreaks of Disease*, 111–142.
© 2001 *Kluwer Academic Publishers.*

information *on all outbreaks* of infectious diseases and similar occurrences caused by toxins that seem to deviate from the normal pattern" without restricting the information exchange to human diseases[1] (emphasis added). But no explicit reference was made with respect to animal and plant pathogens. This holds true also for the recommendations of the *Ad Hoc* Meeting.

The participants of the *Ad Hoc* Meeting, likewise, did not explicitly declare whether *all* types of pathogens and toxins are to be covered. They only decided, *inter alia*, that, "since no universal standards exist for what might constitute a deviation from the normal pattern States Parties are encouraged ... to fully utilize existing reporting systems within the WHO, and ... to provide background information on diseases caused by organisms which meet the criteria for the risk groups III and IV according to the classification in the 1983 WHO *Laboratory Biosafety Manual*, the occurrence of which, in their respective areas, does not necessarily constitute a deviation from normal patterns".[5]

Also with respect to the information to be provided on outbreaks of infectious diseases and similar occurrences, that seem to deviate from the normal pattern, no specific request was made regarding agents or diseases covered. It was merely stated that an "exchange of data on outbreaks that seem to deviate from the normal pattern is considered particularly important in the following cases:

- when the cause of the outbreak cannot be readily determined or the causative agent[a] is difficult to diagnose,
- when the disease may be caused by organisms which meet the criteria for risk group III or IV, according to the classification in the 1983 WHO Laboratory Biosafety Manual,
- when the causative agent is exotic to a given region,
- when the disease follows an unusual pattern of development,
- when the disease occurs in the vicinity of research centres and laboratories subject to exchange of data under item A[b],
- when suspicions arise of the possible occurrence of a new disease."

By adding the footnote regarding "organisms made pathogenic by molecular biology techniques, such as genetic engineering" the participants of the *Ad Hoc* Meeting took into account the widespread concern that "perhaps the most significant event in the history of biological weapons development has been the advent of biotechnology. It enables the development of new microorganisms and products with new, unorthodox characteristics".[6]

---

[a] "It is understood that this may include organisms made pathogenic by molecular biology techniques, such as genetic engineering". [Footnote in ref. 5]

[b] Subject to exchange of data under item A are facilities "that meet very high national or international safety standards established for handling, for permitted purposes, biological materials that pose a high individual and community risk or specialize in permitted biological activities directly related to the Convention" (5, p. 4).

The *Ad Hoc* Meeting agreed that a special form should be used ("Form 2")[c] "for the exchange of initial was well as annual information" on outbreaks that seem to deviate from the normal pattern "to enable States Parties to follow a standardized procedure".

## 3. Participation of WHO

From the very beginning, the involvement of WHO in collection and evaluation of the data on outbreaks was proposed. Australia, for example recalled that "the WHO has much experience in assessing epidemiological data, and given an adequate data base would identify new or unusual outbreaks of diseases. There would seem no advantage in setting up a parallel organization to assess epidemiological data.... Such an expanded system of data collection would not only build confidence in the BW Convention but would assist in world strategies to control disease".[7] The German Democratic Republic, likewise, proposed to submit information on unusual outbreaks not directly to the UN Department of Disarmament, as decided by the participants of the Second Review Conference, "but primarily to the international institutions in charge of the respective group of agents and/or of diseases, i.e. the World Health Organization (WHO), the Food and Agriculture Organization (FAO) and the Office International des Epizooties (OIE)[d].... At least some of such information is already routinely made available to WHO, FAO and OIE.... These bodies are staffed with experts capable of properly evaluating the information received.... A sound assessment of such information by the United Nations Disarmament Department appears to require the establishment of a specialized sub-department with a competent staff".[8]

In the view of Dr. K. Uemura, then director of the Division of Epidemiological Surveillance and Health Situation and Trend Assessment of WHO, who was invited by the chairman of the *Ad Hoc* Meeting to brief the experts on that issue, WHO would be an appropriate recipient for those reports. The delegations of the United States and of some other States Parties, however, did not want WHO to become involved in the matter.

At least it was decided that the information provided by States Parties should also be made available to the WHO.[5]

---

[c] In the course of modification and amendment of the CBMs by the Third Review Conference in 1991 (see section 5) Form 2 has been renamed "Form B (ii)".

[d] It took ten years before OIE became related to the BWC topics at least superficially: Dr. Katsuaki Sugiura, Charge de Mission, Scientific and Technical Department of OIE, took part in the 8th workshop of the Pugwash Study Group on the Implementation of the Chemical and Biological Weapons Convention: Strengthening the Biological Weapons Convention" in Geneva, September 1997.

#### 4. The Initial Efficiency of the Information Exchange

In 1989 SIPRI launched an evaluation of the first three rounds of the information exchange.[9] The authors of the study came to the conclusion that participation in the CBMs was disappointing both in quantitative and qualitative respects. This held true also for the information on outbreaks of infectious diseases and intoxinations[e].[10] Only a few states gave a little information, not using the forms recommended by the expert group. Only Canada provided background information from the very beginning, covering the years 1972-86. Three additional States Parties joined Canada in providing such information: China (1989), Sweden (1989), and Germany (1991). The United Kingdom was the first country to report on an outbreak deviating from the normal pattern (see below, section 13.4.2), although not using Form 2 developed by the expert group to be used for such reports but providing a copy of the report which had been submitted to WHO.

As the authors of the SIPRI study ascertained, a lot of information on outbreaks, including outbreaks caused by dual-threat agents[f] (DTAs), was submitted by States Parties not to the Department of Disarmament Affairs but to WHO. That underlines the necessity of involving WHO in the system of reporting outbreaks.

#### 5. Decisions of the Third Review Conference

Because of the insufficiency of participation of States Parties in the CBMs, the measures were improved and amended by the Third Review Conference in 1992.[12] In order to increase participation in the information exchange, it was decided to add a "Declaration form on Nothing to Declare or Nothing New to Declare".[12]

With respect to information on outbreaks, nearly identical language was used as in the modalities agreed in 1987. There were three important differences, however: First, it was decided that diseases caused by risk group II agents, should be declared in the background information in addition to group III and IV agents, because some countries include anthrax in their risk group II.

Second, animal and plant diseases were mentioned explicitly in addition with respect to the background information to be provided: "Since no universal standards exist for what might constitute a deviation from the normal pattern, States Parties are encouraged to

---

[e] The language used in the Final Document of the Second Review Conference and all subsequent UN documents "similar occurrences caused by toxins" would always require reference to infectious diseases also when only diseases caused by toxins are mentioned. We wonder therefore whether the term "intoxinations" should be preferred in such instances. As defined in the SIPRI study mentioned above intoxinations are "intoxications caused by toxins" (9, p. 205).

[f] Dual-threat agents (DTAs) are viruses, bacteria, protozoa, fungi and arthropods as well as toxins which are not only naturally dangerous to other living organisms but which can be deliberately used for hostile purposes as biological or toxin weapon agents (11).

fully utilize existing reporting systems *on human diseases as well as animal and plant diseases, where possible, and systems* within the WHO to provide background information on diseases caused by organisms which meet the criteria for risk groups II, III and IV according to the classification in the 1983 WHO Laboratory Biosafety Manual..." (emphasis added).

Third, to enable States Parties to follow a standardized procedure, the conference agreed on a form ["Form B (i)"] to be used for the provision of background information.

There was no change, however, in the request for the reports on unusual outbreaks, i.e. outbreaks caused by animal and plant agents are not specifically asked for except for renaming the form to be used for immediate information on outbreaks deviating from the norm from "Form 2" to "Form B (ii)".

### 6. Decisions of the Fourth Review Conference

The Fourth Review Conference, on the basis of background information on the participation of States Parties in the agreed CBMs prepared by the Secretariat of the conference,[13] decided not to interfere with the then already ongoing work of the *Ad Hoc* Group of States Parties to the BTWC to elaborate a Protocol to the BTWC (see section 7). The Conference, therefore, neither modified nor amended the CBMs and merely emphasized "the continued importance of the confidence-building measures agreed upon at the Second and Third Review Conferences".[14] While the Conference noted, that the information exchange "has contributed to enhancing transparency and building conference", it recognised, "that participation has not been universal, and that not all responses have been prompt or complete.... In this regard, the Conference urge[d] all States Parties to complete full and timely declarations in the future".

### 7. Proposals of the *Ad Hoc* Group

As the Fourth Review Conference noted, "the *Ad Hoc* Group of States Parties established by the Special Conference in 1994 is, as part of its continuing work, considering the incorporation of existing and further enhanced confidence-building and transparency measures, as appropriate, in a regime to strengthen the Convention".[14]

It can be expected that the additional protocol to the BTWC, which is presently being elaborated by an *Ad Hoc* Group, will deal also with reports on outbreaks of disease. There is already agreement that States Parties to the Protocol submit "Declarations". Different opinions are expressed by the members of the *Ad Hoc* Group whether also declarations on outbreaks of disease shall be requested.[15]

In addition it can be assumed that basic elements of the CBMs will be considered in the protocol. According to the table of contents of the rolling text, Article VIII of the protocol covers confidence-building measures. But that article in the October 1998 version of the rolling text is still only an empty page.[15] The rolling text, however, includes several annexes, one of which, Annex G, deals with CBMs.[15] Section IV of that annex deals with "multilateral information sharing ... including electronic networking on issues relating to materials and activities of potential relevance to and in harmony with the BTWC and the legally binding measure".[15] Among the "areas which could be covered" all CBM "reports (as agreed in 1991)" are mentioned, including "Exchange of information on outbreaks of infectious diseases and similar occurrences caused by toxins". As sources for the information on disease outbreaks data from WHO, OIE and FAO are considered, such as *WHO Weekly Epidemiology Record*, WHO EMC's (Division of Emerging and other Communicable Diseases Surveillance and Control) electronic distribution system, *OIE Disease Information, OIE Bulletin, OIE World Animal Health, FAO/OIE/WHO Animal Health Yearbook*, and OIE HandiSTATUS, an electronic information programme containing data related to OIE and FAO/OIE/WHO questionnaires.

## 8. Present State of Participation in the CBMs

Today, when most of the 1998 reports[16] are available[g], the situation is still unsatisfactory with respect to participation of States Parties in the information exchange, although the number of participants, including numerous countries providing information on outbreaks, increased after the Third Review Conference. Nevertheless there are still some 60 States Parties which did not participate in the CBMs until now.

Most participating States Parties took part only once or a few times in the information exchange. Only eight states participated in all rounds of the information exchange as requested by the Second Review Conference and emphasized by the Third Review Conference: Canada, Finland, the Netherlands, Norway, the Russian Federation (and the former USSR), Sweden, the United Kingdom and the United States of America[h].

On the other hand one signatory (Mali) and one non-State Party (Kyrgyzstan) took part in the exchange, although only once each.

Several countries *de facto* participated in the information exchange but merely submitted the nil declaration "Declaration form on Nothing to Declare or Nothing New to Declare for use in the information exchange". Some of these states did not even mark

---

[g] For 1998 only those 41 reports could be evaluated which reached the Department of Disarmament Affairs (DDA) before 10 September 1998 and were disseminated thereafter among States Parties. Until the end of 1998 no additional reports were distributed by DDA, although it can be assumed that some additional reports were received by DDA after 10 September 1998.

[h] But see footnote g.

any of the boxes of the nil declaration with a tick, for example Saint Lucia and San Marino in 1995[i].

Iraq in 1993 and 1996 submitted its reports in Arabic although it was decided by the 1987 *Ad Hoc* Meeting which elaborated the modalities for the reports "that all information agreed ... should be provided *in one of the authentic languages* of the Convention", i.e. in Chinese, English, French, Russian or Spanish (emphasis added).[5]

Occasionally the appearance of the reports was totally unsatisfactory. It was almost impossible, for example, to understand the diseases listed and most figures mentioned in the background information provided by Italy in its 1998 report.

## 9. Availability of Information on Outbreaks

42 countries participated in the information exchange without providing background information or reports on outbreaks (Table 1). It is remarkable that even a depositary of the BTWC, the Russian Federation, did not provide such information, although Russia provided extensive reports on the other items of the information exchange. Some others claimed explicitly that no outbreaks of reportable infectious diseases occurred at all ("nothing to declare") in the period covered, for example Bhutan, Chile, Denmark, Mexico, Qatar, Saudi Arabia, Sri Lanka, Ukraine and others, although Chile had its first outbreak of cholera this century in 1991, and Mexico had large dengue epidemics during that time. Portugal submitted form B (i) uncompleted and designated as "Nil report". Norway, for example, in 1997 (as well as in earlier reports) stated in Form B (i) that "there have been no unusual outbreaks for any of these years, in 1996. Within 'unusual outbreaks' we consider human, animal as well as plant disease" - although in that Form no information on unusual outbreaks but background information on reportable infectious diseases was requested. Norway could have reported cases of human botulism in 1991, 1994 and 1997 (see section 14.7). As there is no reason at all to doubt Norway's compliance with the BWTC, one must conclude from this answer (and from similar responses by other countries) that the title of Form B (i) is ambiguous with respect to the words "reportable infectious diseases".

In the background information some states occasionally provided different figures in different reports. In most cases this was presumably due to updating with retrospectively identified or not confirmed cases. Some of the figures provided by Cuba for the occurrence of *Brucella bovina* cases differ however very much (Table 2). An explanation might be provided by the 1994 report, where figures for both cases and outbreaks are given. Perhaps only the high numbers in Table 2 refer to *cases* while the lower numbers refer to *outbreaks*.

---

[i] It is a matter of opinion whether submission of an incomplete nil declaration can be regarded as "participation in the information exchange". Because the said states have at least responded by provision of the incomplete form they as well some other states have been regarded as participants in tab. 1.

**Table 1    42 states parties participated in the CBMs 1987-1998 without providing background information**

| State | no. of reports | State | no. of reports |
|-------|------|-------|------|
| Armenia | 2 | Panama | 1 |
| Austria | 9 | Papua New Guinea | 1 |
| Bangladesh | 1 | Paraguay | 1 |
| Bhutan | 1 | Peru | 2 |
| Bolivia | 1 | Philippines | 1 |
| Croatia | 1 | Poland | 8 |
| Cyprus | 5 | Portugal | 5 |
| Denmark | 11 | Qatar | 3 |
| Fiji | 4 | Russian Federation & formerUSSR | 12 |
| Greece | 4 | Saint Lucia | 1 |
| Iceland | 3 | San Marino | 3 |
| Kenya | 1 | Saudi Arabia | 2 |
| Korea, Democratic People's Republic | 1 | Senegal | 1 |
| Kuwait | 1 | Seychelles, Republic of | 1 |
| Kyrgyztan[j] | 1 | Sri Lanka | 1 |
| Lao People's Democratic Republic | 1 | Thailand | 1 |
| Luxembourg | 4 | Togo | 1 |
| Mali[k] | 1 | Tunisia | 1 |
| Mexico | 2 | Turkey | 7 |
| Nicaragua | 1 | Uganda | 1 |
| Norway | 12 | Yugoslavia | 1 |

**Table 2    Occurrence of *Brucella bovina* cases in Cuba according to different background reports**

| Rept. | 1988 | 1989 | 1990 | 1991 | 1992 | 1993 | 1994 | 1995 | 1996 | 1997 | 1998 |
|-------|------|------|------|------|------|------|------|------|------|------|------|
| 1993 | 2522 | 2353 | 2486 | 1339 | 3975 | | | | | | |
| 1994 | | | | | | 3056[l] | | | | | |
| 1995 | | | 168 | 172 | 216 | 232 | 229 | | | | |
| 1997 | | | | | | 232 | 229 | 275 | 297 | | |
| 1998 | | | | | | | 229 | 275 | 297 | n/d | 3934 |

Altogether only 39 States Parties provided background information on infectious diseases and intoxinations (Table 3). The completeness of that information was very variable, too. Belarus, for example, in 1995 and 1996 mentioned one disease, cholera,

---

[j] Neither State Party nor signatory

[k] Signatory

[l] In the 1994 report 3056 *cases* are declared and 41 *outbreaks* of *Brucella bovina*.

which was also reported on form B (ii) as an outbreak deviating from the norm. The Czech Republic mentioned only three diseases in a background report. Italy, on the other hand, provided a comprehensive survey and reported on some 50 diseases. The background information provided by Iraq in 1995 was entitled "Effect of embargo on the communicable disease in Iraq".

Romania in 1992 reported on morbidity and provided numbers of cases per 100,000 inhabitants, i.e. 0.09 cases of anthrax in 1988. Regarding animal diseases Romania, in 1995, provided figures on outbreaks and cases, e.g. 1990 anthrax: 5/14.

India in its only report, provided in 1997, used two standards in its background information: Regarding human diseases (and major plant diseases) it provided "background information on outbreaks of Reportable Infectious Diseases", defining "an outbreak of disease" as "an incidence of cases in excess of that expected for the time, place or the season". With respect to animal disease it provided "Background information on incidence of reportable infectious diseases". In consequence, for 1994 one outbreak of plague is reported (and none in 1991-93), but 7609 cases of rinderpest.

Only a few States Parties provided background information on animal and plant diseases and reported on outbreaks.

**Table 3** **39 States parties provided background information on infectious diseases and intoxinations 1987-1998**

| State | reports / background info | State | reports / background info |
|---|---|---|---|
| Argentina | 6 / 2 | Iraq | 4 / 3 |
| Australia | 9 / 7 | Ireland | 6 / 3 |
| Belarus | 5 / 2 | Italy | 8 / 5 |
| Belgium | 4 / 1 | Japan | 9 / 6 |
| Brazil | 6 / 4 | Jordan | 3 / 2 |
| Bulgaria | 7 / 4 | Korea, Republic of | 7 / 6 |
| Canada | 12 / 11 | Malta | 5 / 3 |
| China | 9 / 7 | Mongolia | 5 / 3 |
| Chile | 3 / 2 | New Zealand | 10 / 6 |
| Colombia | 1 / 1 | Romania | 8 / 7 |
| Cuba | 8 / 6 | Slovakia | 5 / 3 |
| Czech Republic & former CSSR | 10 / 3 | Slovenia | 6 / 4 |
| Ecuador | 4 / 1 | South Africa | 5 / 5 |
| Estonia | 5 / 1 | Spain | 10 / 8 |
| Finland | 12 / 5 | Sweden | 12 / 8 |
| France | 9 / 6 | Switzerland | 11 / 7 |
| Germany | 10 / 8 | Ukraine | 6 / 4 |
| Hungary | 9 / 7 | United Kingdom | 12 / 8 |
| India | 1 / 1 | United States | 12 / 7 |
| Iran | 1 / 1 | | |

## 10. Reports on Outbreaks of Human Diseases Deviating from the Norm

Only 11 States parties provided reports on Form B (ii) on outbreaks deviating from the norm: Belarus (1), Belgium (1), Brazil (2), Cuba (4), Iraq (1), the Islamic Republic of Iran (6), the Netherlands (8), the Republic of Korea (2), Romania (1), Switzerland (2), and the United Kingdom (3). Although it was explicitly requested that, "in order to enhance confidence, *an initial report* of an outbreak of an infectious disease or a similar occurrence that deviates from the normal pattern *should be given promptly* after cognisance of the outbreak and should be followed up by annual reports",[5] which request was repeated by the Third Review Conference,[12] none of the outbreaks was announced immediately (emphasis added).

Most outbreaks reported because they deviated from the norm were obviously caused by agents not thought to be major putative warfare agents such as BSE prions, polioviruses and measles virus. Polio and measles outbreaks were reported by the Netherlands; they affected people who refused vaccination for religious reasons.

Belarus, Brazil, the Islamic Republic of Iran, and the Republic of Korea, respectively, reported on outbreaks of cholera caused by contaminated water, food, or imported from abroad. Iran, in addition, provided information on outbreaks of typhoid fever.

Sweden, in 1992, reported on 27 cases of legionellosis caused by *Legionella pneumophila*. The disease occurred in the Hospital of Vørnamo, spreading into several separate wards of the hospital. The outbreak stopped when the temperature in the hot water system was increased from $+45^{\circ}C$ to $60^{\circ}C$.

Throughout the period of 12 years covered by this review only one report described an outbreak deviating from the norm because it was allegedly caused by a violation of the BTWC (see section 12).

## 11. Reports on Outbreaks of Animal Diseases

Regarding outbreaks in animals, Australia, for example, in 1997, i.e. in her report covering 1996, provided information on a major outbreak of anthrax in dairy cattle in the Goulburn Valley in central northern Victoria early in 1997 (see below, subsection 13.1.2). Sweden and the United Kingdom also reported on outbreaks of anthrax (see below, subsection 13.1.2).

The Islamic Republic of Iran reported an outbreak of foot-and-mouth disease in 1996 (see subsection 13.7.2). The Netherlands reported an outbreak of hog cholera. The disease affected three pigs in 1992 and was presumably caused by illegal swill feeding.

The UK reported in 1993 on an outbreak of blue-eared pig disease, which was first recognised on 16 May 1991 (i.e. 2 years before the report was provided). According to the report blue-eared pig disease is a new disease caused by a virus, probably by an arterivirus. It was first recognised in North America in 1987 (but not reported on within the CBMs) and in continental Europe late in 1990. At the time of the report 237 confirmed cases were recognised. According to the report it is unknown how the disease reached Europe and how it entered England: "It has been suggested that industrial sabotage motivated the deliberate introduction of the agent to infect a competitor company. There is no evidence to support this theory which, in any case, seems improbable as it was almost as likely to affect the perpetrator's pigs as those of the target company". This conclusion is drawn because the agent can be spread either by the movement of affected, but often clinically normal, pigs or by the airborne route. In the view of the authors of the report it is "more probable ... that the agent was accidentally introduced with an illegal importation of genetic material of some kind".

## 12. Reports on Plant Diseases

Within the framework of its 1997 report, dated 24 April 1997, Cuba on Form B (ii) reported the occurrence of *Thrips palmi* in December 1996, a dangerous plant pest (and at the same time vector of phytopathogenic viruses) so far not encountered in Cuba. Cultures of potatoes, beans, paprika, eggplants, cucumber, pumpkins and other crops had been affected. Regarding the suspected source it was emphasized that an US aircraft overflew the country two months before the insects were first detected.

Four days later, on 28 April 1997, Cuba sent a *Note verbale* to the Secretary General of the United Nations,[17] reporting the appearance of *Thrips palmi* in Cuba and relating it to the dropping of an unknown substance by an US aircraft overflying Cuba on 21 October 1996. The Cuban note concluded that "there is reliable evidence that Cuba has once again been the target of biological aggression". The accusation was categorically denied by the United States.

In June 1997 Cuba requested a consultative meeting to consider the problem. The meeting was held in Geneva on 25-27 August 1997. Statements were made both by Cuba and the United States. Cuba provided additional evidence supporting its claims and the US denied these allegations and discussed possibilities of how *Thrips palmi* might have reached Cuba as a consequence of natural processes.

The report of the formal consultative meeting recorded that "States Parties welcomed the fact that the delegations of Cuba and the US sought to clarify their positions with respect to the concerns raised by the Government of Cuba".[18] However, since not all matters had been fully resolved by the meeting, it was suggested that States Parties submit additional comments and that the chairman of the meeting report in writing on the final outcome of these consultations.

Comments were submitted by 12 States Parties expressing, not unexpectedly, quite different views on whether the Cuban allegation could be substantiated or not. The chairman's report in consequence concluded, that "due *inter alia* to the technical complexity of the subject and the passage of time it has not proved possible to reach a definitive conclusion with regard to the concerns raised by the Government of Cuba".[19]

Iraq, in 1991, reported on a disease affecting 92,754 date palms, causing a deformation and rot of the crown of growing plants. As possible causative agents *Thielaviopsis*, date-palm fossorial insects, were mentioned.

## 13. Reports on Diseases of "Most Concern"

It would be beyond the scope of this chapter to deal with the reports of diseases caused by all of the numerous biological agents and toxins regarded to be dual-threat agents and listed, for example, in the rolling text of a Protocol to the BTW. In the October 1998 draft of the Rolling Text, for example, 30 human pathogens (16 viruses [2 in brackets][m], 9 bacteria [4 in brackets], 3 rickettsiae [1 in brackets], and 2 protozoa [in brackets] and 19 toxins [12 in brackets] are listed, as well as 14 animal pathogens [all but one, rinderpest virus, in brackets] and 18 plant pathogens [all in brackets].[15]

We will restrict our analysis in the following sections, therefore, to agents and toxins which are, in the most recent view of the US Department of Defense "of most concern".[20] That assessment was made in 1997, when it was decided to initiate the "Joint Vaccine Acquisition Program" to create stockpiles of licensed vaccines for use by the US military. Agents and toxins causing the following 12 infectious diseases and intoxinations are "of most concern": anthrax, brucellosis, plague, Q fever, tularemia; encephalitides caused by alphaviruses (Eastern equine encephalitis, Venezuelan equine encephalitis, Western equine encephalitis), smallpox; botulism, intoxinations caused by ricin and by Staphylococcal enterotoxins, respectively.

In addition reports on the occurrence of foot-and-mouth disease and rinderpest (cattle plague) will be mentioned here because the possible use of their causative viruses as BW agents was assessed during World War II.[21] Rinderpest virus is the only animal pathogen which is included in the lists of the most recent rolling text without brackets.

## 13.1 ANTHRAX

### 13.1.1 Background Information
*Human anthrax*. 20 countries which provided background information did not mention anthrax at all, although it is universally present in the soil.

---

[m] Square brackets indicate a divergence of views between delegations participating in the Ad Hoc Group as to the language that should be used and/or to the items covered.

Five countries, namely Australia[n], Finland, Ireland, Jordan, and Sweden, explicitly reported zero cases of anthrax.

Several States Parties provided background information on the occurrence of anthrax:

Bulgaria (5 to 11 cases annually)
China (866 to 2527)
Germany (0 to 2)
Hungary (0 to 2)
Japan (usually 0 cases, 2 each in 1992 and 1994)
Mongolia (0 to 4)
Netherlands (usually 0 cases, 2 in 1993)
Romania (0.02 to 0.09 per 100,000 population)
South Africa (0 to 4)
Switzerland (0 to 1)
Ukraine (3 to 38)
United Kingdom (0 to 3)
USA (0 to 2).

*Animal anthrax.* Several States Parties provided background information on the occurrence of anthrax in animals:

Germany (0 to 1 cases annually)
India (1139 to 2627 cases in 1991-95)
Japan (0 to 1)
Mongolia (2 to 153)
Netherlands (0 to 1)
Romania (4/5 to 21/25 outbreaks/cases)
South Africa (16 and 333 cases in 1995 and 1994, respectively)
Switzerland (0 to 2)
United Kingdom (1- 5).

Australia reported on "exceptional occurrences, confined to certain regions".

*13.1.2 Outbreaks of Anthrax deviating from the Norm*
As already mentioned, Australia on 16 April 1997 and in the following year provided information on a major outbreak of anthrax in dairy cattle in the Goulburn Valley in central northern Victoria early in 1997. The first case was diagnosed on 26 January. Since recording began in 1914 anthrax had never occurred in that area. During the following weeks anthrax was detected at 82 further farms, affecting 202 cattle and four sheep. There was also one human case, a knackery (slaughterhouse) worker infected with the cutaneous form who recovered uneventfully, following antibiotic therapy.

---

[n] In Australia, human anthrax has not been notifiable since 1991.

Since an outbreak of anthrax of this size was quite unusual in Australia detailed epidemiological investigations were carried out. As described in the 1997 report, all outbreaks occurred in intensively irrigated pastures. The irrigation paddocks concerned had been recently regraded and the irrigation channels cleaned and reconstructed. High humidity, aggravated by increased irrigation efficiency, exceptionally high temperatures and soil disturbance are all thought to have contributed to this unusual outbreak. It was considered, that anthrax occurred in the affected region in the last century "in association with stock routes, knackeries and boiling-down works. Soil in the area had been disturbed over recent years by major earthworks to improve irrigation efficiency and to remake channel and drainage systems". Measures to counter the disease included burning the carcasses of infected animals, vaccinating all other animals in the affected herd and all cattle in the area. The site was disinfected with 5% formaldehyde, a buffer zone was established, and affected properties were quarantined.

It is not obvious why this important information - a quite unusual outbreak caused by one of the most suspicious DTAs - was given as one of the "Comments on selected List B diseases" and was not provided on a form B(ii). Of course it is to be welcomed that information was provided immediately.

The Netherlands in 1992 reported an outbreak of anthrax in the second half of 1991 affecting ten cattle in the Groningen Province. The suspected cause of the disease was contaminated animal bone-meal feed.

The United Kingdom in 1993 reported on form B(ii) on an outbreak of anthrax at a single intensive breeding-fattening pig farm in Wales. There were 19 confirmed cases. The outbreak probably was caused by contaminated feed, but this assumption could not be confirmed. "The outbreak lasted over 3 months on the affected unit. This was most unusual".

13.2 BRUCELLOSIS

*13.2.1 Background Information*
*Human brucellosis.* Several States Parties provided background information on the occurrence of brucellosis in humans:

Argentina (486 and 722 cases in 1992 and 1993, respectively)
Australia (16 to 46 cases annually)
Bulgaria (2 cases in 1995)
Canada (2 to 20)
China (253 to 1888)
France (71 to 204)
Germany (21 to 43)
Hungary (0 to 2)
Iraq (667 to 14,989)
Ireland (6 to 159)
Italy (1119 to 1571)

Japan (0 to 1)
Jordan (750 and 770 cases in 1993 and 1994, respectively)
Malta (1 to 18)
Netherlands (1 to 10)
New Zealand (3 to 30)
Romania (morbidity in 1997: 0.004 per 100,000 population)
South Africa (1 to 37)
Spain (7 to 42)
Sweden (1 to 5 cases during 1985-89°)
Switzerland (16 to 37)
USA (75 to 120).

*Animal brucellosis.* Some states reported on brucellosis affecting cattle or other animals:

Australia (no cases since July 1989)
Cuba (168 to 6364 cases annually, but see section 13.2.2)
Germany (1 to 45)
Japan (0 to 1)
Mongolia (616 in 1993 and 6634 to 53,019 in 1988-92)
Romania (6/17 to 15/357 outbreaks/cases)
South Africa (7596 cases in 1994)
Switzerland (one case each in 1988 and 1996).
United Kingdom (no cases in 1988-96)

### 13.2.2 Outbreaks of Brucellosis Deviating from the Norm
No outbreaks deviating from the norm of human or animal brucellosis were reported, although the occurrence of quite different numbers of cases in Cuba (see Table 2) must have been exceptional.

There were also some years with exceptionally high numbers of cases in humans in China and Iraq and in animals in Cuba, Mongolia and Romania (see above).

### 13.3 PLAGUE
### 13.3.1 Background Information

15 countries, namely Australia, Canada, Finland, France, Germany, Hungary, India, Ireland, Japan, Netherlands, Republic of Korea, South Africa, Sweden, Switzerland, and the United Kingdom, explicitly reported zero cases of plague.

---

° Not notifiable since 1990

Background information on the annual occurrence of plague was provided by:

> Brazil (0 to 26 cases annually)
> China (3 to 84)
> India[p] (1 in 1994)
> Mongolia (1 to 21)
> USA (2 to 17).

### 13.3.2 Outbreaks of Plague Deviating from the Norm

No outbreaks of plague deviating from the norm were announced by any of the countries participating in the information exchange, although the plague in India was clearly abnormal (see section 14.2).

### 13.4.  Q FEVER

### 13.4.1. Background information

Information on the occurrence of Q fever was given by:

> Australia (353 to 860 cases annually)
> Bulgaria (9 to 66)
> Germany  (40 to 166)
> Hungary (0 to 14 cases)
> Italy[q] (14 to 35)
> Netherlands (15 to 30)
> Romania (0 to 0.11 cases per 100,000 inhabitants)
> Slovakia (0 to 127)
> Slovenia (2 in 1991)
> Spain (0 to 4)
> Switzerland (10 to 53).

### 13.4.2. Outbreaks of Q Fever Deviating from the Norm

The United Kingdom in 1990, reported an outbreak of Q fever by adding a report submitted to WHO in September 1989 as part of the weekly "Communicable Disease Report" routinely sent to the WHO. During the period May to July 1989, more than 100 patients with acute *Coxiella burnetti* infection were diagnosed at East Birmingham Hospital. Other laboratories in the West Midlands also noted an increase in Q fever cases. A case-control study did not reveal a common source for the infections. As there was "seasonal coincidence of the outbreak with the lambing period of sheep, and as the summer has been early and relatively dry, wind-borne contaminated dust from lambing areas around Birmingham [was] being considered as a likely source of the outbreak".

---

[p] India defined in its only report, provided in 1997, an outbreak of disease as "an incidence of cases in excess of that expected for the time, place or the season". The number refers to outbreaks, not cases.

[q] Not notifiable since 1992

There was no explanation, however, why predominantly older males of working age (with a mean of 53 years) were affected.

In contrast to the modalities agreed the report was not provided using form B[r], and the information was not provided immediately.

## 13.5 TULAREMIA

### 13.5.1. Background Information
Information on the occurrence of tularemia was given by:

> Canada[s] (1 to 58 cases in 1973-82)
> Estonia (0 cases in 1991-97 except for 24 in 1996)
> Finland (5 to 560)
> Germany (0 to 5)
> Hungary (32 to 106)
> Italy (3 to 56)
> Netherlands (no case since 1988)
> Slovakia (17 to 152)
> Spain (no cases in 1991-96, one in 1997).
> Sweden (0 to 133)
> Switzerland (0 to 2)
> Ukraine (2 to 4)
> USA[t] (96 to 201 in 1988-94).

### 13.5.2 Outbreaks of Tularemia Deviating from the Norm
No outbreaks of tularemia deviating from the norm had been reported by any States Party, although Canada, Estonia, Finland, Hungary, Italy, Slovakia and Sweden all had some years with exceptionally large numbers of cases (above).

## 13.6 EASTERN, VENEZUELAN AND WESTERN EQUINE ENCEPHALITIS

### 13.6.1 Background Information
Almost no background information on occurrences of Eastern (EEE), Venezuelan (VEE) and Western equine encephalitis (WEE) - caused by closely related alphaviruses - was provided except by Canada (but see section 14.4). Whereas no data are available in Canada on the occurrence of EEE and VEE at least since 1972 and on the occurrence of WEE since 1979, it was reported that during 1972-78 0 to 14 cases of WEE occurred annually.

---

[r] Now Form B (ii)

[s] No data available since 1983.

[t] No longer notifiable in the USA since 1995.

128

Some states provided background information on encephalitis caused by other agents:

> Australia (no cases of Australian encephalitis[u] 1991-97, except two cases in 1996)
> China (1984-87 207 to 270 cases of "forest spring encephalitis" and 18,282 to 29,065 cases of Japanese encephalitis; 1988-97 4751 to 21,189 cases of "epidemic encephalitis")
> Germany (397 to 1665 cases of "viral encephalitis")
> Hungary (206 to 329 cases of tick-borne encephalitis; in addition 70 to 124 cases of *encephalitis infectiosa*)
> India (0 to 2 cases of Japanese encephalitis in 1991-94)
> Ireland (0 to 10 cases of "acute encephalitis")
> Japan (4 to 55 cases of Japanese encephalitis)
> Malta (1 person died from acute viral encephalitis in 1996)
> Mongolia (no cases of Japanese encephalitis in 1988-94)
> Republic of Korea (0 to 4 cases of Japanese encephalitis)
> Romania (morbidity in 1997: 0.08; reported as unusual outbreak in 1997)
> Slovakia (51 to 102 cases of viral encephalitis)
> Switzerland (27 to 370 cases of tick-borne encephalitis)
> USA[v] (in 1988-94 680 to 1341 primary infections and 82 to 170 cases of post infectious encephalitis).

The USA could have quoted its summaries of arthropod-borne virus activity in humans and animals which appear annually in the CDC's *Morbidity & Mortality Reports*. These complement the totals for primary viral encephalitis given in the USA report. In addition, the Pan American Health Organization collects statistics for EEE, VEE and WEE in all countries of the Americas.

*13.6.2 Outbreaks of Encephalitis Deviating from the Norm*
Not a single outbreak of Eastern, Venezuelan or Western equine encephalitis was reported.

Romania in 1997 reported an outbreak of acute encephalitis, meningitis and menigoencephalitis caused by a flavivirus, West Nile virus. 527 cases were clinically suspected; 168 laboratory confirmed by serological tests. Nine persons died. (West Nile virus does not belong to the agents "of most concern", nor is it included in the list of human pathogens of the rolling text of a protocol to the BTWC.)

---

[u] Australian encephalitis is caused by Murray Valley encephalitis virus and Kunjin virus, which are flaviviruses.

[v] No longer notifiable in the USA since 1995.

## 13.7 FOOT-AND-MOUTH DISEASE

### 13.7.1 Background Information
Background information on the occurrence of foot-and-mouth disease (FMD) was provided by:

> India (24,342 to 203,041 cases in 1991-95)
> Iran (0 cases in 1993-95, 480 and 165 cases in 1996 and 1997 respectively)
> South Africa (one case in 1995).

The Pan American Health Organization publishes statistics for FMD in all the countries of the Americas, from data provided by the countries, so the information is certainly available. Colombia, Ecuador and Venezuela were infected with FMD in 1998. Argentina and Paraguay were last infected in 1994, Brazil in 1996, and Uruguay in 1990.[22]

Germany, the Netherlands, South Africa, Switzerland, and the UK explicitly reported no cases of FMD.

### 13.7.2 Outbreaks of Foot-and-Mouth Disease Deviating from the Norm
In 1998, the Islamic Republic of Iran reported an outbreak of FMD which occurred in December 1996. The outbreak was caused by FMD virus type A, presumably introduced from Afghanistan with imported cattle. 565 cattle were infected. To contain the outbreak mass vaccination was performed.

In addition, the 1995 case reported by South Africa in 1996 was clearly abnormal, as were the 203,041 cases in India.

## 13.8 RINDERPEST

### 13.8.1 Background Information
Rinderpest is endemic in many African countries south of the Sahara. The disease also occurs in the Middle East and in southwestern and central Asia. Records of outbreaks in recent years are available from the OIE. But India was the only country which provided background information on the occurrence of rinderpest: 5556, 1903, 1614, 7609, and 676 cases of rinderpest occurred there in the years 1991-95.

### 13.8.2 Outbreaks of Rinderpest Deviating from the Norm
No outbreaks of rinderpest deviating from the norm were reported on by any of the States participating in the CBMs, although the occurrence of 5556 and 7609 cases in 1991 and 1994, respectively, in India was clearly abnormal.

## 13.9 SMALLPOX

WHO has established the occurrence of human-to-human transmission of monkeypox in the former Zaire, and considers it to be an emerging disease.[23] It would be useful to include reports of any orthopox virus outbreak in the reports.

## 13.10 BOTULISM

### 13.10.1 Background Information
Background information on botulism was provided by:

> Argentina (2 to 66 cases annually)
> Australia (0)
> Bulgaria (5 to 196)
> Canada (1 to 16)
> Estonia (0 to 11)
> France (8 to 30)
> Germany (4 to 28)
> Italy (12 to 58)
> Netherlands (0)
> Romania (0.02 and 0.09 cases per 100,000 population in 1996 and 1995)
> Spain (2 to 8)
> Sweden (0 to 2)
> Switzerland (usually 0 to 1, 12 cases in 1993)
> USA (84 to 143).

### 13.10.2 Outbreaks of Botulism Deviating from the Norm
Switzerland, in 1994, reported on an outbreak of botulism in the city of Sion in 1993. 12 persons were affected; the intoxination resulted from the consumption of contaminated uncooked air-dried ham. 196 cases in Bulgaria might also be considered unusual.

## 13.11 OTHER INTOXINATIONS

Several states reported registered cases of food poisoning (food-borne diseases) other than botulism and salmonellosis.

### 13.11.1 Background Information
Background information on staphylococcal food poisoning (staphylococcosis) was provided by:

> Czech Republic (525 to 630 cases of "*Staphyloc.* and *Clostr. perf.* food poisoning")
> Hungary (16 to 116)
> Slovenia (121 and 86 cases in 1996 and 1997, respectively).

In addition, background information on unspecified food-borne diseases was provided by:

> Argentina (2364 to 3051 cases annually)
> Cuba (6555 to 14,548)
> Ecuador (266 cases in 1966)
> France (103 to 486 cases)
> Ireland (43 to 275)
> Jordan (268 to 549)
> Malta (1 to 85)
> Netherlands (427 to 1197)
> New Zealand (518 and 67 cases in 1995 and 1996, respectively)
> Romania (8.2 to 13.2 per 100,000 population)
> Slovakia (249 to 553)
> Slovenia (23 to 38)
> South Africa (6 to 502)
> Spain (909 to 1017).

*13.11.2 Outbreaks of Food-Borne Diseases Deviating from the Norm*
Sweden in 1992 reported an outbreak of food poisoning, affecting 342 persons in 1991 using the ferry boat Helsingborg-Helsingør. The suspected source of the intoxination was meat contaminated by *Salmonella agona*. "The infection was spread via the main dishes". While "the opinion at SBL's department for epidemiology [was] that the cause of the infections was inadequate reheating of the food, which made growth of bacteria possible ... the District Infectious Diseases Specialist [suspected] an unnatural cause and made a report of the incident to the police". In any case, "ferry Salmonella has been picked up 'all over' the kitchen".

## 14. Outbreaks Not Reported But Which Should Have Been[*]

### 14.1 ANTHRAX

In July 1997 an outbreak of anthrax affected eight lions (four died) belonging to a European circus performing in Amman, Jordan. Other animals belonging to the circus did not show any sign of the disease. The infection resulted from ingestion of a contaminated donkey carcase which had been obtained from the outskirts of Amman (area of Manara or Baqa'). These were the first cases of anthrax in Jordan since 1992.[24]

### 14.2. PLAGUE

Although India in 1994 officially reported the occurrence of at least 55 fatalities from plague (52 from Surat city and three from New Delhi), with laboratory confirmation of several cases,[25] unequivocal confirmation was never obtained from human specimens. A

---

[*] Our review is intended to be indicative, not necessarily comprehensive.

1998 review by experts from the All India Institute of Hygiene and Public Health, Calcutta, concludes that "the outbreaks of illness that resembled plague during late 1994 in Beed district and Surat were certainly not due to plague".[26] But WHO regulations require the immediate reporting of even suspect cases of plague. Therefore the approximate number of primary cases, total cases and deaths should have been reported on Form B (ii). The figure of "1 outbreak" does not fulfil the requirements.

## 14.3 Q FEVER

In France, a outbreak of Q fever was recognised between March and June in Briaçon, a town in a breeding area in the Hautes Alpes[27]. 29 cases were identified. Exposure to the slaughterhouse site at Briaçon was presumably the main risk factor, with airborne transmission of *Coxiella burnettii*. A confounding factor might have been the consumption of raw meat.

In Germany, an outbreak of Q fever occurred in the small rural town Rollshausen and neighbouring towns in spring 1996.[28] At least 49 residents of Rollshausen, i.e. 16 percent of the inhabitants, became infected, 35 of whom met a clinical case definition of Q fever. A large sheep farm was the presumed source of the outbreak, and the transmission of *C. burnettii* was presumably airborne. Other outbreaks occurred in 1992 in Berlin (80 cases) and 1993 in Hessen (121 cases).[29]

In Spain between 1990 to 1996 ten outbreaks of Q fever occurred, three of which were quite large (14, 11 and 48 cases).[29] Not only were these outbreaks not reported promptly or on Form B (ii), the numbers of cases deviate also from the numbers given in the Spanish background reports.

## 14.4 ENCEPHALITIS

In 1993 and 1996, substantial outbreaks of VEE were reported in the south of Mexico, and in 1995 there was a massive outbreak of VEE, with both human and animal cases, on both sides of the Colombia-Venezuela border.[30] In 1993-95, human cases of VEE were detected in the Amazon region of Peru.[31]

In 1996, EEE in horses was reported from 35 ranches in Mexico. In 1997, five outbreaks of EEE in horses were reported to OIE by Mexico.[32]

The USA reported 132 confirmed or probable human cases of arboviral encephalitis (including cases of EEE and WEE) in 1996, and provisionally 154 cases in 1997, and several cases in horses and farmed emus in 24 states in these two years, in CDC's weekly reports.[33] These should have been included in their CBM returns.

## 14.5 FOOT-AND-MOUTH DISEASE

The following States Parties and other countries, which are usually free of FMD, reported to OIE unexpected outbreaks of the disease[x] in 1996-97 (34):

> Albania
> Greece
> Kyrgyzstan (not a State Party, but which, however, participated once
>    in the information exchange)
> Macedonia
> Swaziland (cattle and buffalo)
> Taiwan (swine)
> Thailand
> Turkey
> Zimbabwe (cattle and buffalo).

## 14.6 RINDERPEST

The following countries, which are usually free of rinderpest, reported to OIE unexpected outbreaks of the disease in cattle in 1996-97[35]:

> Mali (a signatory)
> Niger
> United Republic of Tanzania (a signatory, which had been free of
>    rinder-pest for 14 years)
> Togo

## 14.7 BOTULISM

Norway could have reported two cases of botulism in 1991, one case in 1994 and eight in 1997.[36] Since there were no reported cases as far back as 1982, nor in the intervening years, those would certainly also qualify as deviating from the norm.

Poland could have reported that it had from 107-328 cases of botulism per year from 1990-96.[36] In Hungary and Portugal during 1990-92 botulism accounted for 7% of all reported outbreaks of food-poisoning.[36] Taiwan could have reported two cases in 1993, one in 1994 and three in 1995.[36] Russia could have reported 12 cases of botulism, including one death, in Irkutsk in 1997, due to eating smoked and salted fish.[37]

In Italy an outbreak of botulism took place involving 58 cases, with at least one death. The figure was provided by Italy in her 1998 background information although the outbreak, which was caused by internationally distributed mascarpone soft cheese, would qualify as "deviating from the norm" since it involved 40% more cases than any year since 1991.[38]

---

[x] In cattle unless otherwise noted.

## 14.8 (STAPHYLOCOCCAL) FOOD POISONING

The United Kingdom could have provided background information on staphylococcal food poisoning, since its occurrence during 1969-90 is described in the scientific literature.[39]

Occurrence of cases of food-borne disease, including staphylococcal intoxination, in Japan and the Republic of Korea,[40] Mexico,[41] Poland,[42] and Singapore[43] is also reviewed in the literature.

The following countries which did not provide any information on staphylococcal food poisoning outbreaks deviating from the norm could have done so, since reports are in the literature:

> Canada 1989 (lobster source)[44]
> Germany 1991[45]
> Russia 1996 (children's institutions)[46]
> Taiwan 1994[47]
> Thailand 1990 (400 people at a sports event)[48]
> United Kingdom 1992-93[49]
> United States 1989 (outbreak due to consumption of canned mushrooms imported from the People's Republic of China),[50] 1990 (centralized school lunch provider),[51] 1990 (prison outbreak)[52], 1997 (retirement party).[53]

## 14.9 HANTAVIRUS PULMONARY SYNDROME

In 1993 in the southwestern United States there was an outbreak of a lethal respiratory disease, later called hantavirus pulmonary syndrome. The syndrome is an exciting and at the same time frightening example of the threat of emerging diseases.[54]

The disease which at the beginning of the outbreaks involved American Indians ("Navajo flu")[55] seemed originally to be centered at the junction of four southwestern states[y] ("Four Corners Disease"). Through November 1993, 45 cases of the syndrome had been reported in 12 US states, mainly in Arizona and New Mexico, 27 of whom died.[56] Scientists of the Centers for Disease Control and Prevention, Fort Collins, CO, and the US Army Medical Research Institute of Infectious Diseases (USAMRIID), Fort Detrick, MD, were able within weeks to discover that the disease was caused by a hitherto unknown hantavirus called "Sin Nombre virus". The virus was spread by the contaminated excreta of deer mice (*Peromyscus maniculatus*) the population of which exploded in that region of the USA in early 1993.[57]

---

[y] Arizona, Colorado, New Mexico and Utah

As the agent causing the syndrome had been unknown thus far it is not (yet) a dual-threat agent, though there has been speculation that the virus might have escaped from USAMRIID or other facilities of the US Army.[58] Another hantavirus, the virus causing Korean haemorrhagic fever, is known to be a DTA. Sin Nombre virus is mentioned in the rolling text,[15] in the list of human pathogens, although in brackets.

In the 1994-96 US reports hantavirus pulmonary syndrome is mentioned. In 1994, 53 cases are reported for 1993 for the period between May 1 through December 31 on Form B (i) as background information. It is explicitly stated, however, in the 1994 nil declaration ("Declaration form on nothing to declare or nothing new to declare ..."), that there is "nothing to declare" with respect to measure B (ii) for 1993.

In the 1995 report *no* cases are reported for the period 1990-94 in form B (i). Information in Form B (ii) on outbreaks of infectious diseases that seem to deviate from the normal pattern is not provided. There are three publications dealing with the new hantavirus mentioned, however, in the list of publications attached to the report.[59]

In 1998, 32 (1994) and 23 (1995), 22 (1996) and 18 (1997) cases of hantavirus pulmonary syndrome are reported in form B(i); these figures differ slightly from the numbers given in the 1997 and 1996 reports due to updating with retrospectively identified cases.

## 14.10 AMNESIC SHELLFISH POISONING

Late in 1987 an outbreak of "amnesic shellfish poisoning" occurred in Canada. 165 people suddenly became ill after eating cultured blue mussels. Four of them died, and 12 who survived suffered permanent memory loss reminiscent of Alzheimer's disease.[60] In order to evaluate the outbreak and its origin a special task force was created and an entire analytical laboratory was dedicated to the work. More than 100 people were involved in the elucidation of the accident.[61] They finally discovered that the poisoning was caused by mussels that had accumulated an algal neuro-toxin.[62]

Canada neither reported this immediately nor did it mention the outbreak and its source in its following annual reports (i.e. the 1988, 1989 and 1990 reports) and Canada did not mention the reports dealing with the intoxination in their annual reports on publications. Canada, instead, informed the *Ad Hoc* Committee on Chemical Weapons of the Conference on Disarmament on 3 August 1989 of this intoxination. Canada indicated that the outbreak "bears many similarities to the situation that might be expected from a clandestine attack using such a novel agent".[63] One expert concluded: "While there was never any suggestion that this particular event may have been due to a hostile act, the challenge faced by the investigative team was much like the challenge posed by the hostile use of a novel toxin or toxicant weapon".[61]

## 15. Comments

One possible indicator for violations of the BTWC or the Geneva Protocol is the occurrence of infectious diseases or intoxinations deviating from the norm. This is why the participants of the Second and Third Review Conference of the Parties to the BTWC agreed to request States Parties to provide background information on outbreaks of infectious diseases caused by risk group II, III and IV agents and intoxinations on an annual basis and to report immediately on outbreaks that seem to deviate from the normal pattern.

This study confirms earlier conclusions that the reporting on outbreaks is insufficient both quantitatively and qualitatively - not to mention the still relatively low level of over-all participation in the CBMs:

* 42 countries participated in the information exchange without providing information on outbreaks, which in fact occurred in several of them..
* Only 39 States Parties provided background information on infectious diseases and intoxinations, and only to an extremely variable extent.
* Only 11 States Parties provided reports on outbreaks deviating from the normal pattern, although such deviations were reported by many other countries elsewhere.
* None of the reports on outbreaks was provided immediately.
* Numerous outbreaks caused by dual-threat agents "of most concern" were not reported according to the modalities agreed, although they were reported to WHO or elsewhere.

When it was decided by the Second and Third Review Conferences that States Parties are to report, *inter alia*, on outbreaks of infectious diseases and intoxinations, it was one of the first, rather weak attempts to strengthen the BTWC by confidence-building measures. In the meantime the VEREX process has taken place and the *Ad Hoc* Group (AHG) of the States Parties to the BTWC has been working since 1995. The AHG has made much progress in elaborating a rolling text of a Protocol to the BTWC which, *inter alia*, is destined to promote and to demonstrate compliance with the BTWC. The future protocol to the BTWC will include in all likelihood provisions for dealing with outbreaks. These provisions will then override the existing reporting mechanism under the CBMs for those States Parties to the BTWC, which are also States Parties to the Protocol. However, the CBMs should stay in force for all the BTWC States Parties which have not ratified the future Protocol.

The modalities for the exchange of information on outbreaks should be modified, however.

## 15.1 PROPOSED MODALITIES FOR PROVISION OF BACKGROUND INFORM-ATION

According to the present modalities the background reports are only of very limited value. First, some of the "diseases of most concern" are not or no longer notifiable in some countries. That holds true, for example for alphavirus-caused encephalitis (EEE, VEE, and WEE) and tularemia in Canada, human anthrax in Australia, human brucellosis in Sweden, Q fever in Italy, tularemia and encephalitis in the USA.

Second, there were very great differences in the numbers of infectious diseases and intoxinations declared in the background reports. States Parties reported a range of from 50 (Italy), to one (Belarus) and zero diseases (Denmark and others).

Third, only a few of the diseases reported are caused by dual-threat agents (DTAs) which are listed in the rolling text, and only a few of them are "agents of most concern". Of the about 40 diseases declared by the USA in 1998, for example, only 5 are caused by DTAs, four of which are "agents of most concern".

It would be useful, therefore, not only to develop a specific form for background reports on outbreaks, such as Form B (i) as agreed by the Third Review Conference,[12] but to develop and distribute forms where those diseases which are of most concern are already mentioned in the left hard column, i.e. diseases caused by the agents mentioned in the rolling text.[15] These forms could be distributed by the Department of Disarmament Affairs and, later, by the secretariat of the BTWC Organization, annually to all States Parties with the request for immediate completion. That would require not too much expenditure but would certainly act as a reminder and contribute to enhance the number of returns.

## 15.2 PROPOSED MODALITIES FOR PROVISION OF REPORTS ON OUT-BREAKS DEVIATING FROM NORMAL PATTERNS

More informative than background information are reports on outbreaks that seem to deviate from the norm, especially if the outbreaks seem to be caused by a DTA. But even such reports are of little value if they are - in contrast to the decisions of the 1987 *Ad Hoc* Meeting and of the Third Review Conference - not provided immediately but only once a year together with the background document.

States Parties should be energetically requested therefore to provide - at least provisional - reports of outbreaks immediately. Full use should be made by States Parties and the (future) BTWCO secretariat of outbreak information available on the Internet, particularly that on ProMED-mail,[64] which is recognized as an independent source of reliable reports on human, animal and plant diseases, which are usually confirmed later by the responsible international organisations after the time-consuming process of official notification from the governments concerned[z].

The office of each State Party responsible for reporting these CBMs should liaise closely with the Ministries of health and agriculture to ensure the provision of correct and current information.

These considerations for modification of these modalities might be also taken into account by the AHG in the course of completing the CBMs as attached to the Protocol of the BTWC.

## 16. Acknowledgements

The work of E. Geissler was generously supported by the Volkswagen-Stiftung. The work of J. Woodall was supported by the National Research Council of Brazil.

## Notes

1   United Nations (1986) *Final Document.* PART II. *Final Declaration*, Second Review Conference of the Parties to the Convention on the Prohibition of the Development, Production and Stockpiling of Bacteriological (Biological) and Toxin Weapons and on their Destruction. 30 September, BWC/CONF.II/13/II, 6.

2   Meselson, M., Guillemin, J., Hugh-Jones, M., Langmuir, A., Popova, I., Shelokov, A. and Yampolskaya, O. (1994) The Sverdlovsk anthrax outbreak of 1979, *Science* **266**, no. 5188, 1202-08.

3   Guillemin, J. (1999) Detecting anthrax. What we learned from the 1979 Sverdlovsk outbreak. *This volume.*

4   Australia, Canada, France et al. (1986) Proposal. Article V, in United Nations (ref. 1), PART III. *Report of the Committee of the Whole.* BWC/CONF.II/13/III, 20.

5   United Nations (1987) *Report, Ad Hoc* Meeting of Scientific and Technical Experts from States Parties to the Convention on the Prohibition of the Development, Production and Stockpiling of Bacteriological (Biological) and Toxin Weapons and on their Destruction. 21 April, BWC/CONF.II/EX/2.

6   US Department of Defense (1986) *Biological Defense Program*, Report to the Committee on Appropriations, House of Representatives, Washington, DC, May, 1-7.

7   Australia (1987) Measures for the exchange of information and data, in United Nations (ref. 5), Attachment, 2-3.

8   German Democratic Republic (1987) WHO and other agencies as recipients of information on item 4 (b), in United Nations (ref. 5), Attachment, 28.

---

[z] Information on ProMED-mail and how to subscribe is provided on the following website: <http://www.healthnet.org/programs/promed.html>.

9   Geissler, E. (ed., 1990) *Strengthening the Biological Weapons Convention by Confidence-Building Measures*. SIPRI Chemical & Biological Warfare Studies no. 10. Oxford University Press, Oxford.

10  Woodall, J.P. and Geissler, E. (1990) Information on outbreaks of infectious diseases and intoxinations, in Geissler (ref. 9), 105-24.

11  Geissler, E, and Woodall, J.P. (eds., 1990), *Control of Dual-Threat Agents: The Vaccines for Peace Programme*, SIPRI Chemical & Biological Warfare Studies no. 15. Oxford University Press, Oxford.

12  United Nations (1981) *Final Document. PART II. Final Declaration*. Third Review Conference of the Parties to the Convention on the Prohibition of the Development, Production and Stockpiling of Bacteriological (Biological) and Toxin Weapons and on their Destruction. BWC/CONF.III/23/II. Geneva, 9-27 September.

13  United Nations (1996) Background information on the participation of States Parties in the agreed confidence-building measures (CBMs). 1992 - 1996. Status as of 26 August 1996. BWC/CONF.IV/2. 28 October.

14  United Nations (1996) *Final Document. PART II. [Final Declaration]*. Fourth Review Conference of the Parties to the Convention on the Prohibition of the Development, Production and Stockpiling of Bacteriological (Biological) and Toxin Weapons and on their Destruction. BWC/CONF.IV/L.1/Add.1. 5 December, 6.

15  United Nations (1998) Rolling Text of a Protocol to the Convention on the Prohibition of the Development, Production and Stockpiling of Bacteriological (Biological) and Toxin Weapons and on their Destruction , *in Procedural Report of the Ad Hoc Group* of States Parties to the Convention on the Prohibition of the Development, Production and Stockpiling of Bacteriological (Biological) and Toxin Weapons and on their Destruction, PART I. ANNEX I, BWC/*AD HOC* GROUP/43, 6-283.

16  United Nations (1987-98) BWC/CONF.III/2 and Add.1, 2 and 3; DDA/4-92/BWIII and Add.1, 2, 3, 4, and Report of Romania; ODA/9-93/BWIII and Add.1 and 2; CDA/16-94/BWIII and Add.1 and 2; CDA/14-95/BW-III and Add.1, 2 and 3; CDA/11-96/BW-III and Add.1 and 2; CDA/BWC/1997/CBM and Add.1; DDA/BWC/1998/CBM and Add.1.

17  United Nations (1997), A/52/128, 29 April, quoted in G.S. Pearson (1997) Cuban allegation of BW attack, *The ASA Newsletter* no. 97-5 (17 October), 1, 12-13.

18  United Nations (1997) BWC/CONS/1, 29 April, quoted in Pearson (ref. 17).

19  Quoted by G. Pearson, G. (1998) Cuban allegation of BW attack: the Final Report, *The ASA Newsletter*, no. 98-2 (30 April), 28.

20  US Department of the Army (1987), Joint Program Office for Biological Defense Request for Proposal DAMD17-95-R-5020 for manufacture of defense vaccines, quoted by J. Melling (1999) Vaccine Production, in A. Kelle, M. Dando, and K. Nixdorff (eds.), *The Role of Biotechnology in Countering BTW Agents*, Dordrecht, Kluwer Academic Publishers, forthcoming.

21  Geißler, E. (1999) *Biologische Waffen - nicht in Hitlers Arsenalen. Biologische und Toxin-Kampfmittel in Deutschland von 1915 bis 1945*. 2nd ed., LIT-Verlag, Münster.

22  Pan American FMD and Zoonosis Center (1998) *Monthly Epidemiological Report* **30**, no. 10 (October).

140

23 CDC (1997) Human monkeypox -- Kasai Oriental, Democratic Republic of Congo, February 1996-October 1997. *MMWR Morb. Mortal. Wkly. Rep.* **46**, no. 49 (12 December), 1168-71.

24 OIE (1997) Emergency report - Text of a fax received on 21 August 1997 from Dr M.M.Amarin, Director of the Veterinary Department, Ministry of Agriculture, Amman, Jordan. *OIE Disease Information* **10**, no. 34.

25 Gushulak, B.D., St. John, R., Jeychandran, T., and Coksedge, W. (1994) Human plague in India, August-October 1994, *Can. Commun. Dis. Rept.* **20**, no. 20 (30 October), 181-83.

26 Deodhar, N.S., Yemul, V.L. and Banerjee, K. (1998) Plague that never was: a review of the alleged plague outbreaks in India in 1994, *J. Public Health Policy* **19**, no. 2, 184-99.

27 Armengaud, A. et al. (1997) Urban outbreak of Q fever, Briaçon, France, March to June 1996. *Eurosurveillance* **2**, no. 2 (February), 12-15.

28 Lyytikäinen, O. et al. (1997) Outbreak of Q fever in Lohra-Rollshausen, Germany, spring 1996, *Eurosurveillance* **2** no. 2 (February), 9-11.

29 Editorial (1997) Q fever in Europe. *Eurosurveillance* **2** no 2 (February), 13-15.

30 WHO (1995) Outbreak of Venezuelan equine encephalitis in Colombia and Venezuela, *Wkly. Epidemiol. Rec.* **70**, no. 40, 283.

31 Watts, D.M., et al. (1998) Venezuelan equine encephalitis febrile cases among humans in the Peruvian Amazon River region, *Am. J. Trop. Med. Hyg.* **58**, no. 1 (January), 35-40.

32 OIE (1996) *OIE Disease Information*; OIE (1997), *OIE Disease Information* **10**, no. 42.

33 CDC (1998) Arboviral infections of the central nervous system -- United States, 1996-1997, *MMWR Morb. Mortal. Wkly. Rep.* **47**, no. 25 (3 July), 517-22.

34 OIE, *OIE Disease Information*.<http:/www.oie.int>.

35 OIE (ref. 34); United Nations Food and Agriculture Organization (1997). *Press Release.* 97/5.

36 Berger, S.A. (1998), GIDEON software program version 98-4, CY-Informatics, Ltd, Ramat Hasharon, Israel.

37 Itar-Tass (1997) An outbreak of botulism in the Irkutsk region of the Federation of Independent States, 31 July .

38 WHO (1996), Food safety - outbreak of botulism, Italy, *WER/REH [Weekly Epidemiological Record]* **71**, no. 49 (5 December), 374.

39 Wienecke, A..A., Roberts, D., and Gilbert, R.J. (1993) Staphylococcal food poisoning in the United Kingdom, 1969-90, *Epidemiol. Infect.* **110**, no. 3, 519-31.

40 Lee W.C, Sakai ,T., Lee, M.J., Hamakawa, M., Lee, S.M., and Lee, I.M. (1996) An epidemiological study of food poisoning in Korea and Japan., *Int J Food Microbiol* **29**, no. 2-3 (April), 141-48.

41 Parrilla-Cerrillo, M.C., Vazquez-Castellanos, J.L., Saldate-Castañeda, E.O., and Nava-Fernandez, L.M. (1993) [Outbreaks of food poisonings of microbial and parasitic origins]. [Article in Spanish] *Salud Publica Mex* **35**, no. 5 (September-October), 456-63.

42 Przybylska, A. (1990) [Foci of outbreaks of food poisoning and intestinal infections in Poland 1945-1989]. [Article in Polish] *Przegl Epidemiol* **44**, no. 4, 309-16.

43 Goh, K.T. (1987) Surveillance of food poisoning and other food-borne diseases in Singapore, *Ann. Acad. Med. Singapore* **16**, no. 4 (October), 577-82.

44 Sweet, L., Blackmore, N., and Haldane, D. (1989) Outbreak of staphylococcal foodborne illness related to consumption of lobster -- Nova Scotia, *Can. Dis. Wkly, Rep.* **15**, no. 15 (April), 81-83.

45 Zastrow, K.D., and Schoneberg, I. (1993) [Outbreaks of food-borne infections and microbe-induced poisonings in West Germany 1991]. [Article in German] *Gesundheitswesen* **55**, no 5 (May), 250-53.

46 Solodovnikov, Iu.P., Lytkina, I.N., Chistiakova, G.G., Volkova, L.A., and Parshina, E.I. (1996) [Food poisoning in a boarding school]. [Article in Russian] *Zh Mikrobiol Epidemiol Immunobiol* no. 4 (July), 121-122; Solodovnikov, Iu.P., Lytkina, I.N., Pozdeeva, L.I. (1996) [An unusual epidemic outbreak of food poisoning in a children's health-promotion camp]. [Article in Russian] *Zh Mikrobiol Epidemiol Immunobiol* no. 2 (March), 121-22.

47 Pan, T.M., Chiou, C.S., Hsu, S.Y., Huang, H.C., Wang, T.K., Chiu, S.I., Yea, H.L., and Lee, C.L. (1996) Food-borne disease outbreaks in Taiwan, 1994, *J. Formos. Med. Assoc.* **95**, no. 5 (May), 417-20.

48 Thaikruea, L., Pataraarechachai, J., Savanpunyalert, P., and Naluponjiragul, U. (1995) An unusual outbreak of food poisoning., *Southeast Asian J. Trop. Med. Public Health* **26**, no.1 (March), 78-85.

49 Cowden, J.M., Wall, P.G., Adak, G., Evans, H., Le Baigue, S., and Ross, D. (1995) Outbreaks of foodborne infectious intestinal disease in England and Wales 1992 and 1993, *Commun. Dis. Rep. CDR Rev.* **5**, no. 8 (21 July), R109-17.

50 Levine,W.C., Bennett, R.W., Choi, Y., Henning, K.J., Rager, J.R., Hendricks, K.A., Hopkins, D.P., Gunn, R.A., and Griffin, P.M. (1996) Staphylococcal food poisoning caused by imported canned mushrooms, *J. Infect. Dis.* **173**, no. 5 (May), 1263-67.

51 Richards, M.S., Rittman, M., Gilbert, T.T., Opal, S.M., DeBuono, B.A., Neill, R.J., and Gemski , P. (1993) Investigation of a staphylococcal food poisoning outbreak in a centralized school lunch program, *Public Health Rep.* **108**, no. 6 (November-December) 765-71.

52 Meehan, P.J., Atkeson, T., Kepner, D.E., Melton, M. (1992) A foodborne outbreak of gastroenteritis involving two different pathogens, *Am. J. Epidemiol.* **136**, no. 5 (1 September) 611-16.

53 CDC (1997) Outbreak of staphylococcal food poisoning associated with precooked ham -- Florida, 1997, *MMWR Morb. Mortal. Wkly. Rep.* **46**, no. 50 (19December), 1189-91.

54 Lederberg, J., Shope, R.E. and Oaks jr., S.C. (eds., 1992) *Emerging Infections. Microbial Threats to Health in the United States.* National Academy Press, Washington, DC; Morse, S., (ed., 1993), *Emerging Viruses.* Oxford University Press, New York and Oxford.

55 Anonymous (1993) Mystery epidemic fatal to 11 in Southwest is linked to rodent urine, *Washington Post*, 5 June, A5; Pressley, S.A. (1993) Navajos protest response to mystery flu outbreak, *Washington Post*, 19 June, A3.

56 Hughes, J.M., et al. (1993) Hantavirus pulmonary syndrome: an emerging infectious disease', *Science* **262** (5 November), 850-51; Altman, L.K. (1993) Virus that caused deaths in New Mexico is isolated, *New York Times*, National, 21 November, 24.

57 Nichol, S.T. et al. (1993) Genetic identification of a hantavirus associated with an outbreak of acute respiratory illness, *Science* **262** (5 November), 914-17; Stone, R. (1993) The mouse piñon nut connection', *Science* **262** (5 November), 833.

58 Horgan, J. (1993) Were four corners victims biowar casualties?, *Scientific American*, **269**, no. 5, 16; Wakefield, J. (1994) Federal researchers untangle web spun by newly emerged pathogens, *US Medicine* **2** (March), 16-17.

59 Childs, J.E., et al. (1994) Serologic and genetic identification of *Peromyscus maniculatus* as the primary rodent reservoir for a new hantavirus in the southwestern United States. *J. Infect. Dis.* **169**, 1271-80. Elliott, L., et al. (1994) Isolation of the causative agent of hantavirus pulmonary symdrome. *Am. J. Trop. Med. Hyg.* **51**, 102-08; Spiropoulos, C.F., et al. (1994) Genome structure and variability of a virus causing hantavirus pulmonary syndrome, *Virology* **200**, 715-23.

60 Barinaga, M. (1990) Amino acids: How much excitement is too much? *Science* **247**, no. 4938, 20-22.

61 Schiefer, H.B. (1991) The verification of allegations of the use of novel chemical or toxin weapons: some practical and critical considerations, in E. Geissler, and R.H. Haynes (eds., 1991), *Prevention of a Biological and Toxin Arms Race and the Responsibility of Scientists*, Akademie-Verlag, Berlin, 329-338, see especially p. 331-332.

62 Bird, C.J., et al. (1988) *Identification of Domoic Acid as the Toxic Agent Responsible for the P.E.I. Contaminated Mussel Incident: A Summary of Work Conducted at the Atlantic Research Laboratory of the National Research Council, Halifax, between 3 Dec. 1987 and 11 Jan. 1988.* Atlantic Research Laboratory Technical Report, no. 56, NRCC no. 28083; Bates, S.S. et al. (1988) *Investigations on the Source of Domoic Acid Responsible for the Outbreak of Amnesic Shellfish Poisoning (ASP) in Eastern Prince Edward Island*, Atlantic Research Laboratory Technical Report, no. 57, NRCC no. 29086.

63 United Nations (1989), CD/CW/WO, 254, quoted in *Chemical Weapons Convention Bulletin*, no. 6 (Nov. 1989), p. 8.

64 Woodall, J. (1998) The role of computer networking in investigating unusual disease outbreaks and allegations of biological and toxin weapons use, *Crit. Rev. Microbiol.* **24**, no. 3, 255-72.

# POSSIBLE PARTICIPATION OF THE STATE RESEARCH CENTRE OF VIROLOGY AND BIOTECHNOLOGY "VECTOR" IN A NATIONAL AND GLOBAL NETWORK FOR DISTINGUISHING OUTBREAKS

SERGEY V NETESOV, AND LEV S. SANDAKHCHIEV

*State Research Centre of Virology and Biotechnology VECTOR,*
*Russian Ministry of Public Health*
*Koltsovo, Novosibirsk Region, Russia*

## 1. Introduction

First of all I would like to thank the Organising Committee of this meeting for invitation of my colleagues and myself with the possibility to discuss problems related to the recognition and prevention of international usage of infectious agents with terroristic or military purposes.

The main feature of infectious diseases comes from their global occurrence and, therefore, the world community has to study these infections and try to develop efficient approaches to their diagnosis, prophylaxis and treatment. This is rather a matter of self-preservation and development.

A new level of comprehension of the danger coming from the infectious diseases has been gained as a result of efforts taken by many scientists and experts of different, especially developed.[1-4] The WHO concept "Health for all in the twenty-first century" emphasises the reduction of the infectious diseases' death rates and the eradication of certain diseases as one of its priorities for all the mankind.

According to WHO data, more than 30 previously not know infectious agents causing diseases such as AIDS, haemorrhagic fevers, hepatitis C and many others, have been identified over the last 20 years. As major causes of these diseases are believed to be the adaptation of naturally existing micro-organisms to humans, their mutability acquired under various prophylactics and therapy methods, the increased migration of the population, and increased number of people with suppressed immunity, and several other factors. Thus, our general 20-30 year old understanding of a stable character of the infectious agents has evolved to the end that they are dynamically changing their properties, including such characteristics critical to practice as pathology, antigenic structure, drug resistance, and others.

Thus, if we get back to the issue of non-proliferation and threat reduction we will have to recognise principle differences of biological weapons from other weapons of mass destruction (MWD): overall occurrence of pathogens in nature; permanent emergence of new human-pathogenic variants of micro organisms; and the availability of public health data on the effect of these agents on the human population in different regions of the world. Certainly, one has to bear in mind that the strains and the incidence data

*M. Dando et al. (eds.),*
*Scientific and Technical Means of Distinguishing Between Natural and Other Outbreaks of Disease,* 143–150.
© 2001 *Kluwer Academic Publishers.*

might have potential for misuse. Therefore, we believe that major efforts aimed at non-proliferation and threat reduction should focus on research centres working with emerging pathogens that might present a source of expertise for potential bioterrorists.

Concluding this part of my report, I would like to again stress the global nature of the issue of the infectious diseases. Therefore, it is impossible to fight them without broader international involvement. Russia's great writer Anthon Chekhov wrote once that "...there is no national science as there is no national multiplication table..." This idea is perfectly illustrated by the situation with the infectious diseases that are successfully covering continents, crossing national boarders, and having no respect for either prosperity or poverty.

## 2. Creation of a Global Network

To my mind a very interesting approach was proposed by American scientists and WHO experts that is to try to join efforts of different nations to create a global network for infectious diseases surveillance and control.[3,5] According to these documents, at the initial phase as many as 15 international centres can be formed in the key regions of the world. These centres would co-ordinate their activities with WHO, with the centres in the US and European countries and relevant national authorities responsible for public health issues. How or to what extent can Russia be involved in international collaboration in infectious research? This is not a simple question because the position of certain circles in the US and those in other Western countries still bear some continuing element of mistrust.[12-15] This implication is that Russia might use international collaboration and Western financial support for possible illicit activities. According to John Holum, US Arms Control and Disarmament Agency Director, there are at least 12 countries that have undeclared offensive biological warfare development programmes. However, I strongly believe that Russia is not the main subject of concern to experts for the compliance with the 1972 BW Convention.

Russia has great potential in the area of infectious disease research as well as development and manufacture of therapeutic and prophylactic preparations at facilities of the Russian Ministry of Public Health, those of BIOPREPARAT and local public health establishments. Two major State Research Centres of the Russian Ministry of Public Health – for Applied Microbiology (Obolensk, European region) and Virology and Biotechnology VECTOR (Koltsovo, Eastern region) – before 1990 were involved in biological defence programs of the former Soviet Union and so have years of experience in bacterial defence and viral pathogen research. With their technical and staff capabilities they could play a significant role with the global network for the infectious disease control. Certainly, in considering this issue one has to work out conditions that would completely alleviate concerns over possible non-compliance with the 1972 Biological Weapons Convention.

I would like to remind the audience that Russia has done significant legislative work to strengthen the regime of compliance with 1972 BW Convention and the guidelines of the Australia Group and the BWC Review Conferences:

1) In 1992 a presidential decree on ensuring the fulfilment of international obligations in the area of biological weapons[6] was constituted.

2) Procedures for controlling the export from the Russian Federation of disease agents, their genetically altered forms and fragments for genetic material were introduced.[7] Relevant amendments were made to the Russian Criminal Code.[8]

3) Committees on export and currency control as well as a Committee on the issues of Biological and Chemical Weapons Conventions Compliance at the office of the Russian President were formed. Relevant instructions were elaborated and introduced by the Russian Ministry of Public Health and the State Customs Committee.

In its activities, our Centre completely follows these guidelining documents and forwards annual reports to the Committee in the issue of Biological and Chemical Weapons Conventions Compliance at the office of the Russia President, which is envisaged by the Review Conference of the 1972 BW Convention, for subsequent submission to the UN.

Our Centres (Obolensk and Koltsovo) are actively involved through the Russian Ministry of Science and Technologies, the Russian Ministry of Public Health in broad international collaboration under such programs as International Science and Technology Centre (ISTC), U.S. National Academy of Sciences (NAS), Association for the promotion of co-operation with scientists from New Independent States of the FSU (INTAS), Civilian Research and Development Foundation (CRDF), Initiatives for Proliferation Prevention (IPP-DOE), National Aeronautics and Space Administration (NASA), Defence Advanced Research Projects Agency (DARPA) which are aimed at non-proliferation and threat reduction by strengthening the confidence building measures and transparency.

We believe the most adequate concept of international collaboration in the area of dangerous pathogens research was developed in 1997 by an expert group of the US National Academy of Sciences (NAS) under the leadership of Prof. Joshua Lederberg and Dr. John Steinbruner.[9] This document was prepared with the involvement of Russian experts, and it seems to be the most serious analysis of all pros and contras arising from the collaboration in dangerous pathogens research.

In the NAS concept it is envisaged that confidence building measures and transparency be provided in a broader context. In particular, it is envisaged that in each specific project regular access should be provided to the place of performance and necessary information in compliance with the principle of extending active guarantees to counterparts. It is also envisaged that collaborative work between Russia and American scientists be carried out in laboratories of these countries under a separate agreement. The freedom of access is even more vaguely defined in such programmes as CRDF, NASA, DARPA and IPP (DOE) which I can quite understand since the declared goal of these programs is to support activities not involving dual threat technologies.

The experience of our Centre shows that efforts funded by the above mentioned programs involve only a part of personnel and practically do not fully employ the most qualified staff and the high containment laboratories which, however, are of the main concern to experts. I should note that 6 pilot projects concluded under the NAS initiative have involved only 5 percent of staff and high containment available.

Recently, we have been actively discussing this issue with experts from the Russian Ministry of Public Health, the Russian Ministry of Science and Technologies as well as our colleagues from different US agencies, ISTC and those from the International Research Centre "The Joint Institute for Nuclear Research" in Dubna, Moscow Oblast.[11]

## 3. Russian International Centres

We believe it serves the interests of non-proliferation and world-wide public health to create in Russia International Centres for the study of pathogens of viral (Koltsovo) and bacterial (Obolensk) nature as a model to address the work on dangerous pathogens. We believe it is very important the WHO as an international public health authority be involved early in this process to participate in discussing the feasibility and developing the concept of the proposed International Centres.

Under the term International Centre we understand an international organisation established by an intergovernmental agreement like those of already existing ISTC or the Joint Institute for Nuclear Research in Dubna. Only this context will make it possible to achieve all goals of non-proliferation and threat reduction by ensuring the fulfilment of major requirements to transparency and confidence building: free access to the program and the results obtained; free access to all facilities and all staff of the International Centre. A continuous involvement of foreign scientists in work in place is a powerful instrument of confidence building. Therefore, we believe it is critical to include all high containment capabilities and supporting facilities into the International Centre in order to alleviate concerns over possible illicit activity. It may have sense to use documents provided by the Dubna Institute in drawing up charter documents for the proposed International Centres.

The Dubna Joint Institute for Nuclear Research employs 6,000 staff. Of these 4,000 receive support from the Institute's budget. Of these 1,000 are research staff. Of these 1,000 research staff, 400 are foreign researchers working on a contract basis (3 to 5 years).

Another international centre that uses a similar model is CERN, Switzerland. You can judge on what high confidence enjoy the above two institutes, working in a very sensitive area of research (nuclear physics) just by the fact that both these centres are under consideration for the Nobel Prize in Peace.

## 3.1 VECTOR

At this point I would like to introduce to you our State Research Centre of Virology and Biotechnology VECTOR, Russian Ministry of Public Health. Vector is a large research and production complex whose primary activities are focused on basic and applied research in the area of theoretical virology, molecular biology, virology, immunology, aerobiology, epidemiology, biotechnology as well as development and manufacture of preventative, therapeutic and diagnostic preparations. The total area of our research and production facilities amounts to more that 250 thousand square meters; our land property makes 8,000 hectares (19,768 acres). The research and experimental facilities at VECTOR allow work with viruses highly pathogenic for humans at an up-to-date scientific level under conditions of complete biosafety for the involved personnel and the environment.

Several buildings that are designated for work with highly dangerous infections meet special biosafety requirements for the high containment facilities: an air tight external perimeter, negative pressure in the working zone, complete sterilisation of all types of discharge (gas liquid and solid). VECTOR is one of the two scientific and experimental facilities in Russia that mainly focuses on virus infections research. The State Research Centre for Applied Microbiology, Russian Ministry of Public Health (Obolensk, Moscow Oblast), is a similar scientific and experiment institution involved in bacterial infections research. VECTOR and the State Research Centre for Applied Microbiology are the only bases both in Russia and the rest of the NIS countries that allow studies employing highly dangerous pathogens at an up-to-date level. Data on capabilities of our two Centres are available in the INTERNET.[10]

The total amount of employees at VECTOR is 2,098. The research and technical staff of the Centre (1,200) is represented by highly qualified personnel specialising in the field of genetic engineering, molecular biology, virology, theoretical virology, immunology, epidemiology, ecology with and extensive experience in highly dangerous viruses and in production of diagnostic and prophylactic preparations. Of 340 researchers, 157 have Candidate and Doctor of Science's Degrees.

The Collection of Cultures of Micro-organisms available in the Centre comprises over 10,000 deposit entries: various viral strains, including the national collection of variola viral strains and strains of viral BSL-4 pathogens; isolates of viral strains; recombinant viral strains; strains of micro-organisms, including producer strains. The collection received an international recognition in 1995 when it was affiliated with the European Culture Collection Organisation (ECCO).

Vector houses one of the two WHO collaborating centres (WHO Collaborating Centre for orthopox virus diagnosis and repository for variola virus strains and DNA) supplied with all required conditions for work with human highly pathogenic viruses, including variola virus. One of the terms of reference of this WHO Collaborating Centre is to preserve and study the Russian collection of variola virus isolates. The other WHO Collaborating Centre for Smallpox and Other Poxvirus infections is located at CDC in Atlanta (Dr.J.J.Esposito). Research collaboration that is established between these two Centres is promising in terms of pure science and, which is of equal importance, in terms of confidence building.

VECTOR has a Breeding and Holding Facility for laboratory animals, including primates that are used in trials on therapeutic and diagnostic preparations being developed at VECTOR. At this point, our monkey breeding facility is the only one operating farm in Russia.

Facilities for the performance of preclinical and clinical trials of new medicine preparations are available at VECTOR. It is important that Centre has a long-term experience in ecology research. Institute of Aerobiology, which is one of the divisions of the Centre, actively participated in studying the environmental situation in different cities of Kuzbass coal mine region and developed recommendations for diminishing pollution there. This institute continues this study now using for this purpose some modern and tailor-made equipment and modern mathematical basis. VECTOR houses a Chair of Basic Medicine at the Novosibirsk State University which makes it possible to involve students and graduates of the University in work of the International Centre. At VECTOR we have also a Regional Centre for the Prophylaxis and Fight against AIDS located on the territory of a specialized clinical isolation department with biosafety level BL3; at our base, we also house a children's TB hospital.

As objects for research to be carried out at the proposed International Centre could serve arboviruses, including tick-borne encephalitis virus which is endemic in Russia; HFRS virus, Omsk hemorrhagic fever virus; filoviruses: Marbug and Ebola; othopoxviruses: smallpox virus, monkeypox, and cowpox viruses; viruses causing hepatitis A, B, C; paramyxovirus, rabdoviruses, influenza viruses, etc. This list of viruses could be extended by tuberculosis and opistorchiasis – human parasitic disease which affect liver. The latter is endemic in Siberia. It also makes sense to address viruses causing zoonotic and anthropozoonotic diseases critical to public health and veterinary.

Scientific programs of the proposed International Centre can be based on recommendations contained in the Controlling Dangerous Pathogens report of US NAS.[9] Research areas should cover fundamental aspects of genetics, physiology, and infectious disease; development of diagnostic methods; design of drugs and vaccines; epidemiological studies, including the investigation of environmental factors and their effect on rodents and insects; the effect of human behaviour and demography, etc. To my mind, it is also important to carefully address the issue of enrolling the staff in various training and exchange programs. It is critical to also consider the issue of an appropriate handling of micro-organisms.

The special attention would be paid to the investigation of the mass outbreaks of infectious diseases in the region (Asian part of Russia, Mongolia, Central Asian republics – members of C.I.S.; possibly China). This investigation may be conducted using molecular epidemiology approach, which allows to determine the sero- and genotypes of infectious agents, possible source of primary infection and even to distinguish whether it was intentional or non-intentional event. Such investigations may be made on regular basis for a wide list of pathogens, which would be extremely useful for monitoring of the evolution of infectious agents. As a result of this research, the proposed International Centre can have its strategic scientific goal such as making prognosis, based on the data of global monitoring, of what new infections might emerge in the future.

Of course, these are only some baselines for possible scientific programs that will be refined and finalised by the Scientific Councils of the proposed Centres if a positive decision is made that the proposed International Centres be finally established. I will not further dwell on this subject as ISTC has issued a development grant award this year for us to prepare a proposal on developing a final concept of establishing the above-mentioned International Centre.

## 4. Conclusion

In conclusion I would like to address the advantages that come with the creation of the International Centres:

1) Though the process of establishing the International Centres is complex and will take several years, the proposed relationship provides for a long-term strategic collaboration, which is far less subject to political or economic conjuncture fluctuations in Member States.
2) International efforts will provide for the highest level of knowledge and accelerate both the study of dangerous pathogens and the development of state-of the-art public health products for diagnosis, prophylaxis and therapy.
3) The creation of the proposed International Centres will make it possible to join our efforts to gain knowledge that is essential to control potential bioterrorists. It is, however, important to establish a regime of an appropriate dissemination and use of the scientific results obtained that might facilitate possible misuse of biological agents.
4) The proposed International Centres will create zones of openness and transparency to efficiently serve the purposes of non-proliferation, cooperative threat reduction, and emergency preparedness.
5) The proposed International Centres will be able to provide the modern fast diagnostics and monitoring of infectious disease agents in the vast territory of East Europe and Northern Asia which would be extremely helpful for prognosis of evolution and possible emerging of infectious diseases which are endemic here.

## Notes

1. *Infectious disease – a global health threat*. Report of the National Sciences and Technology Council, Committee on Informational Science, Engineering and Technology Working Group on Emerging and Re-emerging Infectious Diseases, 1995.

2. *Emerging Infectiouns. Microbiol threats to health in the United States*, J. Lederberg, R.E. Shope and S.C. Daks, Jf., Ed. National Academy Press, Washington, D.C., 1992.

3. *Emerging viruses*, S.S. Morse, Ed., Oxford University Press, 1993.

4. *EMC Annual Report 1996*, World Health Organization, 1993.

5. The Board of international health, white paper *"America's vital interest in global health"*, USA, 1997.

6. *Decree of the Russian President on ensuring the fulfillment of international obligations in the area of biological weapons, Decree* [1] 390, April 11, 1992.

7. *Procedures for controlling the export from Russian Federation of disease agents, their genetically altered forms, and fragments of genetic material that can be used for developing bacteriological (biological) and toxin weapons*, Nov. 20, 1992, Decision RG [1] 892.

8. *Penalties for crimes against peace and security of mankind: Production or proliferation of weapon of mass destruction*. Sections 355 and 356 of the Russian Criminal Code. 1996.

9. *Controlling dangerous pathogens. blueprint for US-Russian cooperation*. October 27, 1997, National Academy of Sciences.

10. http://www.oecd.org/dsti/sti/s_t/ms/prod/russia/russia2.htm.

11. http://www.jinr.ru.

12. R. Preston. *The Bioweaponeers*. The New Yorker, March 9, 1998, pp. 52-65.

13. C. Wachtel, Armes Biologiques: Le Probleme Russe, *La Recherche*, # 310, Juin, 1998, pp. 37-41.

14. R. Preston. Bio-Warfare-Fiction and Reality, *Genetic Engineering News*, March 1, 1998, pp. 6-39.

15. W. Orent. Escape from Moscow, *The Sciences*, May 22, 1998, pp. 26-31.

# SCIENTIFIC AND TECHNICAL MEANS OF DISTINGUISHING BETWEEN NATURAL AND OTHER OUTBREAKS OF DISEASE: AN OVERVIEW OF THE ARW AND A 2000 POSTSCRIPT

GRAHAM S. PEARSON
*Visiting Professor of International Security,*
*Department of Peace Studies,*
*University of Bradford, Bradford,*
*West Yorkshire BD7 1DP, UK*

## 1. Introduction

The NATO ARW on "Scientific and Technical Means of Distinguishing Between Natural and Other Outbreaks of Disease" was held in the Centre of Epidemiology and Microbiology in the National Institute of Public Health in Prague, Czech Republic on Sunday 18 to Tuesday 20 October 1998 under the co-directorship of Professor Bohumir Kriz, Head of the Centre of Epidemiology and Microbiology and Professor Graham Pearson, Visiting Professor of International Security in the Department of Peace Studies in the University of Bradford, UK. 38 experts participated from 16 countries; 20 from NATO countries (France, Germany, Italy, Netherlands, Norway, UK and USA), 15 from partner countries (Czech Republic, Hungary, Poland, Romania, Russia and the Ukraine) and three from other countries (Brazil, South Africa and Sweden).

The workshop was designed to focus on the scientific and technical means of distinguishing between natural and other outbreaks of disease because an outbreak of disease may be the first manifestation of the use of biological weapons and consequently provisions to address an unusual outbreak were a central issue being addressed by the Ad Hoc Group (AHG). This AHG of the States Parties to the Biological and Toxin Weapons Convention (BTWC) is negotiating a legally binding Protocol to strengthen the effectiveness of and improve the implementation of the Convention. As some States Parties were concerned that any outbreak of disease might result in an investigation under the Protocol, there is a clear need to examine whether there are scientific and technical means of distinguishing between an outbreak of disease arising from natural causes and one arising from other causes such as the use of a biological weapon or an accidental release from non-compliant activity.

Outbreaks of disease are recognised world-wide as presenting a threat to human, animal and plant health as well as to global trade and prosperity. The World Health Organization has recognised that emerging and re-emerging diseases are a priority issue that demands international cooperation and action. This Workshop in October 1998 was very timely as the preceding year had seen the intensification of the negotiations by the Ad Hoc Group in Geneva of a Protocol to strengthen the Biological and Toxin Weapons Convention and had also seen the greater recognition world-wide of the potential

*M. Dando et al. (eds.),*
*Scientific and Technical Means of Distinguishing Between Natural and Other Outbreaks of Disease, 151–167.*
© 2001 *Kluwer Academic Publishers.*

vulnerability to the use of biological materials for terrorist purposes. The Workshop enabled the participants to focus on the critical scientific and technical issue of how outbreaks of disease resulting from natural causes could be distinguished from outbreaks resulting from other causes, which needed to be investigated under a future BTWC Protocol. The potential benefits from the ability to achieve such a delineation -- whether the Protocol for the BTWC or for national and international counters to disease -- were evident.

The ARW was structured so as to start by focussing on the importance of distinguishing between natural and other outbreaks of disease, then considering the diseases of concern and what mechanisms exist for identifying outbreaks. Consideration was then given to the scientific characteristics of natural outbreaks before addressing the technical characteristics of a BW attack whether against humans, animals or plants and how such attacks might differ from a natural outbreak. Consideration was given to outbreaks of human, animal and plant diseases and what their various characteristics; these were aided by descriptions of unusual but natural outbreaks. The approaches to be taken in investigating outbreaks were examined in depth using the anthrax outbreak at Sverdlovsk in 1979 as a case study. Recent advances in biotechnology had enabled techniques such as PCR (polymerase chain reaction) and SCCP (single stranded conformation polymorphism) to be developed which could quickly carry out subspecies differentiation of the pathogens involved in a particular outbreak. This would make it possible to determine whether the subspecies strain involved in the particular outbreak was one which was endemic to the region or was an unusual one not previously found in the region. It was recognised that any investigation of an outbreak needed to be carried out with an appreciation of the normal occurrences of disease within the country of concern. Further presentations focussed on the current networks for the surveillance of disease and on their shortcomings. Consideration was then given to technical contributions to countering outbreaks. Finally, a round table discussion drew together the principal conclusions from the workshop in regard to scientific and technological methods of distinguishing between biological weapons attacks and natural disease outbreaks.

In addition, a special presentation was made on the evening of the first day by Ambassador Tibor Toth, Chairman of the Ad Hoc Group who outlined particular issues relating to the subject of outbreaks of disease that needed to be addressed in the Ad Hoc Group negotiations and the discussions at the ARW might with advantage also examine. These included: legally binding requirements -- as it was necessary to go beyond politically binding requirements, the question was what was realistically possible; reporting and surveillance where much would depend on what information was available on reports of and into outbreaks of disease; delineation between outbreaks arising from natural and unnatural causes was a concern to the NAM; cooperation between a future BTWC organization and the WHO would be important but needed to be explored through quiet discussion; and, scientific & technical cooperation as, because of the dual use nature of pathogens, the strengthening of reporting and surveillance had very important public health benefits, which were extremely important for developing countries and consequently an important scientific and technical cooperation measure for Article X would be the strengthening of global, regional and national elements of reporting and surveillance.

A recurring topic throughout the Workshop was what the relationship would be between the World Health Organization (WHO) (and the other international organisations -- OIE and FAO) and a future BTWC Protocol Organization. It was recognised that the role of the WHO, OIE, and FAO is to promote world wide public, animal and plant health and that to do this effectively the WHO, OIE and FAO had to maintain their neutrality and impartiality. They could not become involved in identification of any suspicious outbreaks of disease -- such identification would be a matter primarily for the States parties to the BTWC and its Protocol and possibly for the future BTWC Protocol Organization. It was, however, vital that the future BTWC Protocol Organization received timely information about outbreaks of disease -- human, animal or plant -- as these occurred if it was to function as an effective professional organization. There was discussion as to how thus might best be achieved. The importance of avoiding dual reporting of disease outbreaks was recognised both from a point of view of the resource implications and from the potential for increased suspicion as a result of discrepancies between data reported through different reporting channels -- there is much to be said for the concept of "one stop shopping" in reporting disease outbreaks by States to international organisations such as WHO, FAO and OIE as well as the future BTWC Organization. There was also detailed consideration about how the future BTWC Organization might obtain and maintain the essential expertise in epidemiology that it will require as the numbers of such experts world-wide are very limited.

The Workshop concluded with a very lively and animated Panel Discussion which addressed a number of issues relating to outbreaks of disease that had been identified in the opening presentations or by Ambassador Toth in his presentation. The issues debated included fell into two major groups: a. Outbreaks of disease, their surveillance and reporting and how natural outbreaks might be distinguished from other outbreaks; and b. Issues relating to the future BTWC Protocol organization, the reporting of disease outbreaks to that organization, the initiation of investigations and the relationship between the BTWC Protocol organisation and other international organisations such as the WHO, OIE and FAO.

## 2. Outbreaks of Disease, their Surveillance and Reporting and How Natural Outbreaks Might be Distinguished From Other Outbreaks

In considering the surveillance and reporting of outbreaks of disease it was recognised that the primary reporting route was undoubtedly to the international organisations responsible for human, animal and plant health -- the WHO, OIE and FAO. There was currently much attention being given to the reporting of emerging and re-emerging infectious diseases to the WHO. However, the requirement for such disease reporting was not more than politically binding upon the member States of the WHO and a parallel situation applied for reporting to both the OIE and the FAO. The advantage in such international reporting lay in the production of collated reports of disease outbreaks around the world which were available to States who could plan their national and regional strategies for countering and preventing disease accordingly. This formal reporting was also usefully augmented by alerting systems such as ProMed which depended on informal links between experts in an increasing number of countries and was an increasingly valuable supplement and complement to the reporting to the WHO, OIE and FAO. The trend for the future lay clearly in the strengthening of national, regional and international reporting of outbreaks of disease to the WHO, OIE and FAO. There was also increased international recognition that because of international travel and trade an outbreak of disease in any country was of concern to other countries. There was much to be said for "one stop reporting" of all disease outbreaks although this was frequently not easy to achieve because different ministries were involved with human, animal and plant disease outbreaks in different countries. The pressure for all countries to report outbreaks of human, animal and plant disease would come from the collated reports of such reports which would indicate which countries had not reported as well as from adjacent States seeking information from its regional neighbours.

It was recognised that once an outbreak is initiated its spread occurs naturally and consequently all outbreaks are "natural" whether arising from a natural occurrence or from a deliberate or accidental initiation of the outbreak. Consequently, the ability to discriminate between an outbreak resulting from a natural occurrence from one arising from other causes will depend on the characteristics of the outbreak, the nature of the disease and whether the pathogen subspecies is one indigenous to the area. It was evident that there is no unique signature that distinguishes an outbreak from other causes from an outbreak resulting from a natural cause as many natural outbreaks have unusual characteristics. The principal distinction would result from a number of contributing aspects -- such as a pathogen that was not endemic to the area, the pattern and location of the outbreaks of the disease which together lead to a persuasive argument that the outbreak had resulted from a cause that was different from a natural occurrence.

3. **Issues Relating to the Future BTWC Protocol Organization, the Reporting of Disease Outbreaks to that Organization, the Initiation of Investigations and the Relationship Between the BTWC Protocol Organisation and Other International Organisations Such as the WHO, OIE and FAO**

Insofar as the future BTWC Protocol organization was concerned, it was recognised that that organization needs to be aware on a continuing basis of the outbreaks of human, animal and plant disease around the world because such an outbreak may be the first manifestation of a non-compliant activity under the BTWC. Much of this information from national, regional and international surveillance is available on the internet and the future Organization would need to access and analyse this information on a regular basis. There was much discussion about whether disease outbreak reporting should be a mandatory measure under the BTWC Protocol building upon the politically binding reporting of disease outbreaks under Confidence-Building Measure B. It was noted that the responses under the CBM had been incomplete and very patchy with great variation between States Parties in what information had been reported under the CBM. In discussion, it was observed that reporting of disease outbreak information through parallel channels to the BTWC Protocol organization on the one hand and to the WHO, OIE and FAO on the other raised the prospect of inconsistencies and hence anomalies and ambiguities between the two sets of reported data. There appeared to be much to be said for putting emphasis on the strengthening of national, regional and international reporting to the WHO, OIE and FAO with consideration given to the copying of such reporting to the BTWC Protocol Organization.

As an outbreak may be the first manifestation of a non-compliant activity under the BTWC, it is clearly essential that the future BTWC Protocol organization is recognised as being a credible professional group that is competent to examine and analyse the available information on outbreaks of disease in humans, animals and plants. As it is probable that field investigations under the Protocol, whether of alleged use or an accidental release from a non-compliant activity, will be extremely infrequent, the epidemiological experts in the future BTWC Protocol organization will need to maintain their expertise through the examination and analysis of the naturally occurring outbreaks of human, animal and plant disease. Such expertise will be invaluable and essential should a State Party request the future BTWC Protocol organization to conduct a field investigation.

As to the initiation of field investigations, it seemed probable that this would be at the request of a State Party -- and would not be initiated by the future BTWC Protocol organization -- because a field investigation, along with facility investigations, would be one of the most political measures available under the Protocol and would not be something that was lightly initiated. It was also clear from the discussion that the onus should be on the requesting State Party to provide persuasive evidence as to why a particular disease outbreak merited a field investigation. It was apparent that evidence that an outbreak was unusual would not, by itself, be sufficient reason for a field investigation. There would need to be other evidence that indicated that the outbreak was not the result of a natural occurrence.

The relationship between the future BTWC Protocol organization and the WHO, OIE and FAO was discussed at some length. It was clear that the international organisations such as the WHO, OIE and FAO need to concentrate on their primary role of improving human, animal and plant health around the world and that this function should not be jeopardised in any way through activities relating to whether or not a country is or is not in compliance with the BTWC. Consequently, the suggestion that the WHO (or the OIE and FAO) might conduct verification activities for the BTWC Protocol Organization appears completely incompatible with the primary function of the WHO, OIE or FAO. In discussion, it appeared probable that the future BTWC Protocol organization would be one of a large number of organisations around the world that look to the WHO, OIE and FAO for information on outbreaks of disease in humans, animals and plants, on how these may be countered and on how public, animal and plant health can be improved. There might well be cooperation between the future BTWC Protocol organisation and the WHO, OIE and FAO in that the future BTWC Protocol organization in its activities to promote international cooperation and technical assistance could well help to increase the understanding and awareness within States Parties of the benefits to those States Parties from improved national, regional and international WHO, OIE and FAO surveillance of and counters to outbreaks of disease. Indeed, the role of the future Protocol organization in promoting increased international cooperation and assistance in improving the national surveillance and reporting of disease outbreaks to the WHO, OIE and FAO could provide an incentive to States to become party to the Protocol.

Overall, it was evident that there were synergistic benefits to countries from a strengthened BTWC through the Protocol and its organisation and improved national surveillance and reporting of disease outbreaks to the WHO, OIE and FAO. Together these would offer the prospect that outbreaks of disease wherever they occurred in the world would be reported and monitored. Over time, the probability that a disease outbreak with suspicious characteristics would not be reported would be reduced thereby maximising the deterrent effect of enhanced outbreak reporting and surveillance bringing benefits to all countries.

The ARW successfully initiated debate on these key issues for the strengthening of the security regime prohibiting biological weapons. Several areas were identified where more detailed investigation of the capability that exists in public, animal and plant health epidemiology could, together with advances in molecular biological techniques which enable the identification of the sub-species strains of organisms causing specific outbreaks, contribute to the differentiation between natural and suspicious outbreaks which was vital for an effective strengthening of the BTWC.

## 4. A 2000 Postscript

The subsequent couple of years has seen considerable development in the Protocol to strengthen the BTWC in respect of those elements relating to field investigations. Many of the square brackets have now been removed through negotiation and it is informative to examine the changes that have taken place in the language that was reproduced in the first chapter[1] of this book.

By December 2000, the draft Protocol[2] language in respect of outbreaks of disease in *Article III G. Investigations* concerning the types of investigations was as follows:

> 3. The requesting State Party shall specify in each request which one
> of the following types of investigation it is seeking:
>
>> 1) Investigations to be conducted in geographic areas where
>> [the release of, or] exposure of humans, animals or plants to
>> microbial or other biological agents and/or toxins has given
>> rise to a concern about possible non-compliance under

Article I of the Convention or alleged use of biological weapons, hereinafter referred to as "field investigations";

(2) Investigations of alleged breaches of obligations under Article I of the Convention, to be conducted inside the perimeter of a particular facility at which there is a substantiated concern that it is involved in activities prohibited by Article I of the Convention, hereinafter referred to as "field investigations";

This is now followed by a section entitled (B) Outbreaks of Disease which contains the following text:

## (B) OUTBREAKS OF DISEASE

[Exclusion of all outbreaks of disease which are due to natural causes]

4. All outbreaks of disease which are due to natural causes do not pose a compliance concern under the Convention and shall not be a reason for an investigation of a non-compliance concern.

5. Nothing in this Protocol shall prejudice the right of a State Party to investigate, as per its national regulations, outbreaks of disease which occur on its territory or in any place under its jurisdiction or control, or if it so wishes, with the assistance of other State(s) and/or relevant international organisations.

*Investigation of a concern that an outbreak of disease is directly related to activities prohibited by the Convention*

6. If a State Party has a concern that an outbreak of disease is directly related to activities prohibited by the Convention, it shall have the right to request a field investigation to address the non-compliance concern. In accordance with the requirements of Annex C, section II, paragraphs 1 and 2, such request shall contain detailed evidence, and other information, and analysis substantiating why, in its view, it considers the outbreak of disease not to be naturally occurring and directly related to activities prohibited by the Convention. [Reports coming from the mass media cannot be considered as evidence.] [Information from private persons cannot be the sole evidence on the basis of which the request shall be made.]

7. The Executive Council shall not [consider a request for] [authorize] a field investigation of an outbreak of disease, unless it determines that there is a basis for concern substantiated by detailed evidence, and other information, and analysis that the outbreak(s) of disease, is not naturally occurring and is directly related to activities prohibited by the Convention. The Executive Council, if it deems it appropriate for its [consideration] [authorisation] of the above request, shall also request from the most relevant international organization(s) such as, but not limited to, the WHO, OIE, FAO, all available information in its/their possession, that may be relevant to the outbreak. When a State Party requests a field investigation of an outbreak(s) of disease on the territory or in any place under the jurisdiction or control of another State Party, the State Party where the investigation is proposed to occur shall have the right to provide evidence, and other information, and analysis that indicates that the outbreak of disease is naturally occurring or otherwise unrelated to activities prohibited by the Convention. If deemed appropriate by the Executive Council as a matter of procedure under Article IX, paragraph 30, other State(s) Party(ies) may also provide information relevant to whether the outbreak(s) of disease is naturally occurring and/or whether it is related to activities prohibited by the Convention. All of the evidence, and other information, and analysis submitted, shall be taken into account by the Executive Council in its consideration of the investigation request in accordance with the request procedures of paragraphs 13 to 28 of this section of Article III.

This language shows that language has been found to address the concern about outbreaks from natural causes being the cause for an investigation. Furthermore, the relationship between the BTWC Protocol organization and the WHO, OIE or FAO has been resolved to one in which the future BTWC Protocol organization requests *from the most relevant international organization(s) such as, but not limited to, the WHO, OIE, FAO all available information... that may be relevant to the outbreak*. However, the earlier NAM and Other States concern about unusual outbreaks of disease is still reflected in paragraph 9 of Article III. G. Investigations which is within square brackets and reads:

*[Unusual outbreaks of disease*

9. The diseases which are endemic in the region and present the expected epidemiological features shall not be considered an unusual outbreak of disease. An outbreak of

disease which appears to be unusual, shall be investigated by the affected State Party, as per guidelines set out in Annex C, section V, and concluded as soon as possible.]

The guidelines set out in *Annex C Investigations* section V are as follows:

*[V. INVESTIGATIONS OF NATURAL AND UNUSUAL OUTBREAKS OF DISEASE*

1. In pursuance of paragraph 9, Article III, section G, an unusual outbreak of disease may be defined as an outbreak which is unexpected within the prevailing and known context for the host agent and environment parameters. For the purposes of this Protocol, an unusual outbreak of disease may have one or more of the following reasons:

(a) That the disease is being reported for the first time in the region and was never known to be endemic;

(b) That the epidemic has occurred outside its normal anticipated season;

(c) That the reservoir host and/or insect vector of the disease do not occur in or were previously eradicated from the affected region;

(d) That the disease appears to be transmitted by an uncommon or unusual route;

(e) That the epidemiological features of the disease suggest increased virulence of the organism manifested in the form of increased case fatality rate;

(f) That the causative agent has higher survival time even in the adverse environmental conditions and shows unusual resistance;

(g) That the causative agent is capable of establishing new natural reservoirs to facilitate continuous transmission;

(h) That the disease occurred in a population with a high level of immunity due to vaccination suggesting that the causative agent has modified;

(i) That the disease is caused by an agent with an unusual population subset or in an unexpected age group;

(j) That the epidemiology of the disease suggests an abnormal reduction in the incubation period of the disease;

(k) That the epidemiology of the outbreak strongly points to environment of a biological agent, but isolation and identification of the suspected agent is not possible by established means;

(l) That the characteristics of the causative agent differ from the known characteristics of that agent prevalent in the territory of the State Party.

2. An outbreak of disease which appears to be unusual may be investigated by the affected State Party to accomplish the following:

(a) Collection of relevant data regarding all aspects of the disease;

(b) Identification of the causative agent;

(c) Characterisation of the causative agent by using molecular techniques such as PCR and DNA sequencing;

(d) Identification of the unusual features of the disease including documentation of the outbreak emphasising on the atypical features;

(e) Assessment of the extent and severity of the outbreak, including the epidemic curve and monitoring of the trends.]

The difficulty with the language in paragraph 9 and the guidelines in Annex C section V are that it ignores the possibility that a biological weapon attack may well choose to use an agent that is endemic within a country as that attack may not be recognised as having been the cause of the disease outbreak. It would be unwise to include such language and guidelines in the Protocol. It is much better to focus on requiring persuasive evidence to be submitted with the request for a field investigation.

The language regarding the information to be submitted by a State Party with a request for a field investigation is now in *Annex C Investigations* and reads as follows:

## (A)  INVESTIGATION REQUEST

*[Detailed] Information [, reasons and evidence] to be submitted with a request for an investigation*

1.  A request for an investigation under paragraph 3 (a) of Article III, section G, for an event(s) which has given rise to a concern about non-compliance shall include the following information:

(a) Name of the State Party[/State] on whose territory or in any other place under whose jurisdiction or control the alleged event(s) has taken place;

(b) If the alleged event(s) has taken place in any place on the territory of a State Party[/State] which is not under its jurisdiction or control, the name of that State Party[/State] (hereinafter referred to as "the host State Party/State");

(c) A description of the alleged event(s), including all [available] information on:

(i) The [use] [release] of microbial or other biological agent(s) or toxin(s) for other than peaceful purposes; and/or

(ii) Weapons, equipment or means of delivery used in the alleged event(s);

(iii) The circumstances under which the alleged event(s) took place;

(iv) The suspected cause and/or perpetrator of the alleged event(s);

(d) To the extent possible, the date and time, when the alleged event(s) took place and/or became apparent to the requesting State Party and, if possible, the duration of that alleged event(s);

(e) The area requested to be investigated in accordance with paragraph 3 below;

(f) Whether any victims are humans, animals or plants as well as an indication of numbers affected and a description of the consequences of exposure, and if so:

(i) Symptoms and/or signs of the disease;

(ii) All available epidemiological data relevant to the disease outbreak;

(g) For requests involving outbreaks of disease, detailed evidence, and other information, and analysis, including detailed information on events [and] [and/or] [or] activities which substantiate its view that an outbreak[(s)] of disease: (a) is not naturally occurring, and (b) is directly related to activities prohibited by the Convention;

[(h)Information from and/or the outcome or results of [any] prior consultations/ clarifications relevant to the request.]

2. In addition to the information to be supplied with a request pursuant to paragraph 1, other types of information may also be submitted as appropriate and to the extent possible including, inter alia:

(a) Reports of any internal investigation including results of any laboratory investigations;

(b) Information on the initial treatment and the preliminary results of the treatment of the disease;

(c) A description of the measures taken to prevent the spread of the disease outbreak and to eliminate the consequences of the alleged event(s), and their results in the affected area, if available;

(d) The request for specific assistance submitted separately in accordance with the provisions contained in Article VI, paragraph 9;

(e) Any other corroborative information, including affidavits of eye witness accounts, photographs, samples or other physical evidence [which in the course of internal investigations have been recognised as being related to the alleged event(s)].

It is evident that the substance of the information to be provided with a field investigation request is now largely out of square brackets. The previous subsequent separate paragraph that sought the provision of information indicating that the outbreak is potentially connected to activities prohibited by the BTWC has now been subsumed into paragraph 1(g) reproduced above.

The December 2000 language in *Article VII Scientific and Technical Exchange for Peaceful Purposes and Technical Cooperation* on measures to promote scientific and technical exchanges has now been considerably expanded and elaborated and now includes:

> *4.     Each State Party shall promote and support, in furtherance of any current endeavours relevant to and in accordance with the Convention, [where appropriate,] individually, jointly, through arrangements, with relevant international organisations and agencies, including, but not limited to, the FAO, ICGEB, IVI, OIE, OPCW, UNEP, UNIDO, WHO and the Secretariat of the CBD, or the institutional mechanisms provided for under section D of this Article:*

> (a) The publication, exchange and dissemination of information, including through workshops, training programmes and conferences, on current and recent developments, as well as on research and development on the peaceful uses of microorganisms and toxins, biosafety, [biodefence,] biotechnology, good laboratory practice and current good manufacturing practice, and diagnosis, surveillance, detection, treatment and prevention of diseases caused by biological agents or toxins, in particular infectious diseases;

> (b) The work of existing laboratories on the prevention, surveillance, detection and diagnosis of diseases caused by biological agents or toxins, in particular infectious diseases, to improve the capabilities of such laboratories and their effectiveness, through, inter alia, the provision of training and technical advice, equipment and reagents;

> (c) The improvement and development of States Parties' capabilities, [including where necessary new laboratories,] upon the specific request of, and in cooperation with, the State Party concerned, in the surveillance, prevention, detection, diagnosis and treatment of diseases caused by biological agents or toxins, in particular infectious diseases, as an integral part of a global effort to improve the monitoring of emerging and re-emerging diseases in humans, animals and plants;

together with:

> (g) Transfer among States Parties of technology for the peaceful uses of genetic engineering, the prevention, diagnosis and treatment of diseases caused by biological

agents or toxins, in particular infectious diseases, and for other relevant fields of biosciences and biotechnology for peaceful purposes;

(h) Participation [on [a [fair and equitable] [non-discriminatory] basis] [and as wide a geographic basis as possible]] at the bilateral, regional or multilateral levels in the application of biotechnology and scientific research and development, for the prevention, surveillance, detection, diagnosis and treatment of diseases caused by biological agents or toxins, in particular infectious diseases;

(i) The establishment and conduct of training programmes on the diagnosis, surveillance, detection, prevention and treatment of diseases caused by biological agents or toxins, in particular infectious diseases;

A subsequent section (D) in Article VII addressing the role of the Technical Secretariat includes the following:

*(d) Develop a framework, including through the voluntary fund and voluntary contributions, for States Parties to support an international system for the global monitoring of emerging diseases in humans, animals and plants, and to support other specific programmes to improve the effectiveness of national and international efforts on the diagnosis, prevention and treatment of diseases caused by biological agents and toxins, in particular infectious diseases;*

A further Article VII section (F) on Cooperative Relationships with other International Organisations and Between States Parties includes the following:

*(F) COOPERATIVE RELATIONSHIPS WITH OTHER INTERNATIONAL ORGANIZATIONS AND AMONG STATES PARTIES*

*26. The Organization may, where appropriate, conclude agreements and arrangements pursuant to paragraphs 22 (j), 32 (l) and 36 (f) of Article IX with relevant international organisations and agencies, including, but not limited to, the FAO, ICGEB, IVI, OIE, OPCW, UNEP, UNIDO, WHO and the Secretariat of the CBD, as envisaged in paragraph 6 of Article IX, to enhance compliance and ensure effective and full implementation of Article X of the Convention and this Article in order to, inter alia:*

(a) Derive the greatest possible synergy in, and benefits from:

...

(v) The collection and dissemination of information on the diagnosis, surveillance, detection, treatment and prevention of diseases caused by biological agents or toxins, in particular infectious diseases;

...

(b) Co-ordinate its activities with those of international organisations and agencies on the peaceful uses of bacteriological (biological) agents and toxins, and on the diagnosis, detection, treatment and prevention of diseases caused by biological agents or toxins, in particular infectious diseases, and raise awareness of and facilitate access to those activities by States Parties to the Protocol;

It is thus evident that there is now comprehensive provision within Article VII for cooperation in respect of the surveillance, reporting , diagnosis, detection, treatment and prevention of diseases caused by biological agents or toxins, with particular emphasis on infectious diseases.

The language in *Annex G Confidence-Building Measures* under *IV. Multilateral Information Sharing* in December 2000 is unchanged from that in October 1998 and continues to contain detail under the following headings:

*3.3   Surveillance of disease outbreaks and unusual disease outbreak reports*

*3.3.1  Surveillance of human disease outbreak and unusual disease outbreak reports*

*3.3.2  Surveillance of animal disease outbreak reports*

*3.3.3  Surveillance of plant disease outbreak reports*

There is, however, new language proposed in July/August 2000 by South Africa in *Article VIII Confidence-Building Measures* which is within square brackets:

*[(A) INVESTIGATION OF OUTBREAKS OF DISEASE*

1.  Each State Party may at its own discretion investigate any outbreak of disease on its own territory or in any other place under its jurisdiction or control.  In the investigation of a disease outbreak it may utilize the support and/or aid

from any international organization or other States Parties/States.

2. A State Party may at its own discretion report the outcome of an investigation of any outbreak of disease or any other information on disease outbreaks to the Organization. ....]

The language that was in the October 1998 version of the Protocol, generally within square brackets, referring to the possible involvement of the WHO/IOE/FAO in relation to outbreaks of disease has now largely disappeared as it is generally appreciated that the WHO/OIE/FAO have no direct role to play in relation to investigations under the BTWC Protocol.

It is also now clear from *Annex C Investigations* of the Protocol that investigations will be carried out by full-time staff from the Technical Secretariat of the BTWC Protocol organization and that trained and qualified ad hoc personnel may also be designated to participate in investigations should the necessary expertise not be available within the Technical Secretariat.

## 5. Conclusion

The ARW entitled "Scientific and Technical Means of Distinguishing between Natural and Other Outbreaks of Disease" held in Prague in October 1998 was timely as the Ad Hoc Group negotiating the Protocol to strengthen the effectiveness and improve the implementation of the BTWC had in 1997 intensified its negotiations. A central measure in the Protocol is the investigation of alleged use, which may first become evident as an outbreak of disease. Consequently, the ability of the ARW to discuss how outbreaks of disease arising from natural causes might be distinguished from outbreaks arising from a deliberate or accidental release of pathogens along with the sensitivity of the NAM and other States that an outbreak of disease should not, by itself, be the cause for an investigation was valuable in enabling all participants to gain a better appreciation of what the scientific and technical issues were. The subsequent elaboration and development of the language in the Protocol has shown that much that was discussed during the ARW has been reflected into improved Protocol language.

## Notes

---

[1] Graham S. Pearson, *The Importance of Distinguishing Between Natural and Other Outbreaks of Disease*, in Malcolm R. Dando, Bohumir Kriz, and Graham S. Pearson (eds), *Scientific and Technological Methods of Distinguishing between Biological*

*Weapons Attacks and Natural Disease Outbreaks,* Kluwer Academic Publishers, Dordrecht, 2001.

[2] United Nations, *Ad Hoc Group of the Parties to the Convention on the Prohibition of the Development, Production and Stockpiling of Bacteriological (Biological) and Toxin Weapons and on their Destruction,* BWC/AD HOC GROUP/54, 18 December 2000.

# Index